ANATOMY OF
RESTLESSNESS

Bruce Chatwin was born in 1940. He worked at Sotheby's and then for the *Sunday Times*. His first book, *In Patagonia*, became an instant classic. It was followed by a series of books notable for their originality and style. He was, as Peter Levi said in the *Independent*, 'the best travel writer of his generation, and one of its deepest writers of any kind'.

by the same author

ANATOMY OF RESTLESSNESS

Uncollected Writings

BRUCE CHATWIN

Edited by Jan Borm and Matthew Graves

PICADOR

First published 1996 by Jonathan Cape

This edition 1997 by Picador
an imprint of Macmillan Publishers Ltd
25 Eccleston Place, London SW1W 9NF
Basingstoke and Oxford
www.macmillan.co.uk

Associated companies throughout the world

ISBN 0 330 350086 2

3 5 7 9 8 6 4

A CIP catalogue record for this book is available from
the British Library.

Typeset by Deltatype Ltd, Ellesmere Port, Wirral
Printed and bound in Great Britain by
Mackays of Chatham PLC, Chatham, Kent

CONTENTS

EDITORS' FOREWORD

It is commonly supposed that Bruce Chatwin was an ingenuous latecomer to the profession of letters, a misapprehension given credence by that now-famous passage in his lyrical autoportrait 'I Always Wanted to Go to Patagonia' where we are told that this indefatigable traveller's literary career began in midstride, almost on a whim, with a telegram announcing his departure for the farthest flung corner of the globe: 'Have Gone to Patagonia'.

Such a view overlooks the fact that, from the late 1960s onwards, Chatwin was already fashioning the tools of his future trade in the columns of periodicals as diverse as the *Sunday Times* magazine, *Vogue, History Today*, and *The New York Review of Books,* and that he continued to do so through every twist and turn of his career, from art expert to archaeologist, to journalist and author, right up until his death in 1989.

These previously neglected or unpublished Chatwin pieces – short stories, travel sketches, essays, articles and criticism – drawn from the pages of reviews, catalogues, literary journals and magazines, and gathered together here for the first time, cover every period and aspect of the writer's career, and reflect the abiding themes of his work: roots and rootlessness, exile and the exotic, possession and renunciation.

The present volume is a selection of the best from a wealth of such 'incidental writing' and is designed to provide a reader's companion to Bruce Chatwin, a 'sourcebook' of material offering invaluable insight into the author's life and work.

With this objective in mind, rather than obey the dictates of chronology, the editors have relied on the inner logic of these texts to guide them in the order of their presentation. Indeed, it is intriguing to see a common thread emerge from such diverse material: a recurring pattern of thought and theme drawing together texts published some twenty years apart. Alongside his more familiar narrative gifts, they show Chatwin to have been a passionate and outspoken reviewer, discerning critic, and audacious essayist, possessed of a restless, inquiring mind.

The selected texts have accordingly been grouped by theme and presented in five overlapping sections. The first, entitled 'Horreur du Domicile', opens an autobiographical perspective on to some of the 'writer's chambers', reflecting at once Chatwin's keen sense of place and his passion for things remote and exotic. The second section, 'Stories', offers the reader a fresh glimpse of Chatwin as a compulsive storyteller, forever treading a thin line between fact and fiction. The third section, 'The Nomadic Alternative', returns to a key theme of Chatwin's work via a synopsis of his first, 'unpublishable' book on nomads, in which the author expounds his distinctive vision of History as an ongoing cultural dialectic between civilisation and its natural 'alternatives': nomad and settler, city and wilderness, society and tribe. The fourth section, 'Reviews', invites the reader to rediscover Bruce Chatwin in the unfamiliar guise of a literary critic, in his role as a forthright, polemical reviewer, and in the fifth and final section, 'Art and the Image-Breaker', the author-to-be anticipates a recurrent theme of the novels when he explores the paradoxical nature of artistic creation; its capacity to liberate and emancipate vying with an antagonistic and insidious tendency to obsess and enslave.

In the same autobiographical essay which described the

Patagonian cradling of his literary vocation, Chatwin revealed that his original, extravagant, but ultimately frustrated ambition had been to write 'a kind of "Anatomy of Restlessness" that would enlarge on Pascal's dictum about the man sitting quietly in a room'. When it came to deciding on a title for the present volume, this memorable phrase seemed a fitting choice for a selection of texts that so admirably expresses Bruce Chatwin's enduring fascination with restlessness.

Jan Born and Matthew Graves
Paris, June 1996

I

'HORREUR DU DOMICILE'

I ALWAYS WANTED TO GO TO PATAGONIA

The Making of a Writer

Bruce is a dog's name in England (not so in Australia) and was also the surname of our Scottish cousins. The etymology of 'Chatwin' is obscure, but my bassoon-playing Uncle Robin maintained that 'chette-wynde' meant 'winding path' in Anglo-Saxon. Our side of the family traces its descent from a Birmingham button-maker, yet there is a dynasty of Mormon Chatwins in a remote part of Utah, and recently I heard of a Mr and Mrs Chatwin, trapeze artists.

By the time my mother married into them, the Chatwins were 'Birmingham worthies', that is to say, professional people, architects and lawyers, who did not go in for trade. There were, however, scattered among my forebears and relatives a number of legendary figures whose histories inflamed my imagination:

1 A nebulous French ancestor, M. de la Tournelle, supposed to have been mixed up in the affair of the Queen's Necklace.
2 Great-great-grandfather Mathieson, who, at the age of seventy-one, won the tossing of the caber at the Highland Games and died promptly of a stroke.
3 Great-grandfather Milward – a man obsessed by money, Germany and music. He was a friend of Gounod and

Adelina Patti. He also handled the affairs of the ninth Duke of Marlborough and came to New York to negotiate the marriage agreement between Consuelo Vanderbilt and the Duke, who later sacked him for 'gross incompetence.' One afternoon, while rummaging through an old tin trunk, I found his court suit and marcasite-handled sword. Dressed as a courtier, sword in hand, I dashed into the drawing room shouting, 'Look what I've found!' – and was told to 'take those things off at once!' Poor Great-grandpapa! His name was taboo. Convicted for fraud in 1902, he was allowed out of prison to die.

4 Cousin Charley Milward the Sailor, whose ship was wrecked at the entrance to the Strait of Magellan in 1898. I have written his story in *In Patagonia*. While British Consul in Punta Arenas de Chile, he sent home to my grandmother a fragment of giant sloth's skin which he had found, perfectly preserved, in a cave. I called it 'the piece of brontosaurus' and set it at the centre of my childhood bestiary.

5 Uncle Geoffrey. Arabist and desert traveller who, like T. E. Lawrence, was given a golden headdress (since sold) by the Emir Feisal. Died poor in Cairo.

6 Uncle Bickerton. Pick miner and bigamist.

7 Uncle Humphrey. Sad end in Africa.

My earliest recollections date from 1942 and are of the sea. I was two years old. We were staying with my grandmother in furnished rooms on the seafront at Filey in Yorkshire. In the house next door lived the Free French, and the men of the Scottish regiment were stationed in dugouts across the street. I watched the convoys of grey ships as they passed to and fro along the horizon. Beyond the sea, I was told, lay Germany. My father was away at sea, fighting the Germans. I would wave at the ships as they vanished behind Flamborough Head, a long wall of cliffs that, if a footnote in the Edition Pléiade is correct, was the starting point for Rimbaud's prose poem 'Promontoire'.

At dusk my grandmother would draw the blackout material across the window, brood over a brown Bakelite radio and listen to the BBC News. One evening, a bass voice announced, 'We have won a great victory.' To celebrate the Battle of Alamein my mother and grandmother danced the Highland fling around the room – and I danced with my grandmother's stockings.

My grandmother was an Aberdonian, but her nose, her jaw, her burnished skin and jangly gold earrings all gave her the appearance of a gypsy fortune-teller. She was, I should add, obsessed by gypsies. She was a fearless gambler who, for want of other income, made a tidy living on the horses. She used to say that Catholics were heathens, and she had a sharp turn of phrase. One rainy day in 1944 we were sheltering in a phone booth when an ugly old woman pressed her nose to the pane. 'That woman', said my grandmother, 'has the face of a bull's behind with no tail to hide it.'

Her husband, Sam Turnell, was a sad-eyed solitary whose only real accomplishment was an impeccable tap dance. After the Battle of Britain he found employment as a salesman of memorial stained-glassed windows. I worshipped him. Towards the end of the war, when we had rented, temporarily, a disused shop in Derbyshire, I acquired from him a love of long walks over the moors.

Because we had neither home nor money, my mother and I drifted up and down England staying with relations and friends. Home, for me, was a serviceman's canteen or a station platform piled with kit bags. Once, we visited my father on his mine-sweeper in Cardiff Harbour. He carried me up to the crow's nest and let me yell down the intercom to the ward-room. Perhaps, during those heady months before the Normandy landings, I caught a case of what Baudelaire calls 'La Grande Maladie: horreur du domicile.' Certainly, when we moved into the grim-gabled house of our own in Birmingham, I grew sick and thin and people wondered if I was going to be tubercular. One morning, when I had measles, my mother rushed upstairs with the newspaper and said, jubilantly, that Japan had surrendered and my father would be coming home. I glanced at the photo of the mushroom cloud and knew something dreadful had happened. The curtains of my bedroom were woven with tongues of orange flame. That night, and for years to come, I dreamed of walking over a charred black landscape with my hair on fire.

I lost teddy bears without a whimper, yet clung tenaciously to three precious possessions: a wooden camel known as Laura, brought by my father from the Cairo bazaar; a West Indian conch shell called Mona, in whose glorious pink mouth I could hear the wish-wash of the ocean; and a book. The book was *The Fisherman's Saint*, an account of Sir Wilfred Grenfell's mission work on the coast of Labrador. I still have it. On the title page is written: 'To Bruce on his 3rd Birthday from the postman at Filey. For when he grows up.' I imagined the book must contain some wonderful secret (which it did not), and it maddened me to have to wait all those years. The usual run of children's books left me cold, and at the age of six I decided to write a book of my own. I managed the first line, 'I am a swallow.' Then I looked up and asked, 'How do you spell telephone wires?'

My first job, while staying in Stratford-on-Avon with my great-aunts Janie and Gracie, in 1944, was to be the self-appointed guide to Shakespeare's monument and tomb in the church. The price was threepence a go. Most of my customers were G.I.'s. Not that I knew who Shakespeare was, except that he was somehow associated with the red brick theatre from whose balcony I would chuck old crusts to the swans. Yet, long before I could read, Aunt Gracie had taught me to recite the lines engraved on the tomb-slab:

> *Bleste be ye man yt spares thes stones*
> *And curst be he yt moves my bones.*

The aunts were spinsters. Janie, the elder and wittier, was an artist. As a young woman she'd lived on Capri and drawn sketches of naked boys. She remembered seeing Maxim Gorki, possibly even Lenin; and in Paris she'd been to a party in the studio of Kees Van Dongen, the Dutch painter. During the Great War she worked, I believe, as a nurse. Perhaps the deaths of so many beautiful youths moved her to paint the canvases of St Sebastian that lay in racks around her studio. She was a tireless reader of modern fiction. Later, she would tell me that American writers wrote better, cleaner English than the English themselves. One day she looked up from her book and said, 'What a wonderful word "arse" is!' – and for the first time I heard the name Ernest Hemingway.

Aunt Gracie was very emotional and very deaf. Her great friend (and my passion!) was the Irish writer Eleanor Doorly, through whom she met members of the Dublin Circle. Her approach to literature was entirely romantic. On summer days we used to sit and read by the Avon. Across the stream was a bank called Wire Brake, which, so she swore, was Shakespeare's bank whereon the wild thyme blew – though I found only nettles and brambles. We read Whitman's 'Song of Myself' from an anthology of poetry called *The Open Road*. We read 'The Windhover' of Gerard Manley Hopkins, and we read from Eleanor Doorly's book on Marie Curie. The story of Curie's self-inflicted radium burns affected me greatly. I also wonder if Aunt Gracie was the last Victorian to threaten a child with the spectre of Bonaparte.

One evening, when I'd misbehaved in the bath, she cried, 'Stop that, or Boney will get you!' – and then drew on a piece of paper a dreadful black bicorn hat on legs. Sometime later, in a nightmare, I met the hat outside Hall's Croft, the home of Shakespeare's daughter, and it opened like a furry clamshell and swallowed me.

I remember, too, the aunts having a lively discussion as to whether *Measure for Measure* was suitable entertainment for a six-year-old. They decided no harm could come of it – and from that matinee on I was hooked. The Stratford theatre kept the back row of stalls unreserved until the day of the performance, and I would cycle through the dawn to make sure of getting a seat. I saw most of the great productions of the late 40s and 50s – with the Oliviers, Gielgud, Peggy Ashcroft, and Paul Robeson as Othello – and these constitute for me the Shakespeare of all time. Having lived the plays as a boy, I can now scarcely sit through one without a sensation of loss.

By 1949 the hard times were over, and one evening my father proudly drove home from work in a new car. Next day he took my brother and me for a spin. On the edge of an escarpment he stopped, pointed to a range of grey hills in the west and then said, 'Let's go on into Wales.' We slept the night in the car, in Radnorshire, to the sound of a mountain stream. At sunrise there was a heavy dew, and the sheep were all around us. I suppose the result of this trip is the novel I've recently published, *On the Black Hill*.

At boarding school I was an addict of atlases and was always being ostracised for telling tall stories. Every boy had to be a 'little Conservative', though I never understood – then as now – the motivations of the English class system. Nor why, on Guy Fawkes Day of 1949, the masters encouraged us to burn on a bonfire an effigy of the Labour Prime Minister, Clement Attlee. I was sad for Mr Atlee, and never, even in my capitalist phase, was I able to vote Conservative.

The Chatwins, coming as they did from the heart of England, were fanatical sailors. The names of their boats were the *Aireymouse*, the *Dozmaree*, the *Greebe*, the *Nereid* and, finally, the *Sunquest*, an 18-ton Bermudian sloop built in the 30s to sail around the world. We only sailed as far as Brittany, and once to Spain. I hated the actual sailing, for I was always horribly seasick – and yet I persevered. After reading an account of the effect of the H-bomb on Britain, my 'life-plan' was to sail away to a South Sea island and never come back.

The first grown-up book I read from cover to cover was Captain Joshua Slocum's *Sailing Alone around the World*. This was followed by John C. Voss's *The Venturesome Voyages of Captain Voss*, by Melville's *Omoo* and *Typee*, then Richard Henry Dana and Jack London. Perhaps from these writers I got a taste for Yankee plain style? I never liked Jules Verne, believing that the real was always more fantastic than the fantastical.

One summer when I was thirteen I went alone to Sweden to talk English to a boy of my age whose family lived in a lovely eighteenth-century house by a lake. The boy and I had nothing in common. But his Uncle Percival was a delightful old gentleman, always dressed in a white smock and sun hat, with whom I would walk through the birch forest gathering mushrooms or row to an island to see the nesting ospreys. He lived in a log cabin lit by crystal chandeliers. He had travelled in Czarist Russia. He made me read Chekhov in Constance Garnett's translation, also Duff Cooper's biography of Talleyrand.

The great English novelists were left unread, but were heard, very much heard – *Oliver Twist, Wuthering Heights, Pride and Prejudice* – on gramophone records, in plummy English voices, as I lay in the Birmingham eye hospital with partial paralysis of the optic nerve – a psychosomatic condition probably brought on by Marlborough College, where I was considered to be a dimwit and dreamer. I tried to learn Latin and Greek and was bottom of every class. There was, however, an excellent school library, and I seem in retrospect to have come away quite well read. I loved everything French – painting, furniture, poetry, history, food – and, of course, I was haunted by the career of Paul Gauguin. For my seventeenth birthday the owner of the town bookshop gave me a copy of Edith Sitwell's anthology, *Planet and Glow-worm*, a collection of texts for insomniacs, to which I can trace a number of literary fixtures – Baudelaire, Nerval and Rimbaud, Li Po and other Chinese 'wanderers', Blake and Mad Kit Smart, the encapsulated biographies of John Aubrey and the seventeenth-century prose music of Jeremy Taylor and Sir Thomas Browne.

For a time I went along with the suggestion that I follow the family tradition and train as an architect; but, because I was innumerate, my chances of passing the exams were remote. My parents gently squashed my ambition to go on the stage. Finally, in December 1958, since my talents were so obviously 'visual', I started work as a porter at Messrs Sotheby and Co., Fine Art Auctioneers, of Bond Street, at wages of £6 a week.

I learned about Chinese ceramics and African sculpture. I aired my scanty knowledge of the French Impressionists, and I prospered. Before long, I was an instant expert, flying here and there to pronounce, with unbelieveable arrogance, on the value or authenticity of works of art. I particularly enjoyed telling people that their paintings were fake. We sold the collection of Somerset Maugham, who, at dinner at the Dorchester Hotel, told a story about a temple boy, himself and a baby elephant. On Park Avenue, a woman slammed the door in my face, shouting, 'I'm not showing my Renoir to a sixteen-year-old kid.'

The high points of my fine arts career were:

1 A conversation with André Breton about the fruit machines in Reno.
2 The discovery of a wonderful Tahiti Gauguin in a crumbling Scottish castle.
3 An afternoon with Georges Braque, who, in a white leather jacket, a white tweed cap and a lilac chiffon scarf, allowed me to sit in his studio while he painted a flying bird.

In the summer holidays I travelled east, as far as Afghanistan, and wondered if I was capable of writing an article on Islamic architecture. But something was wrong. I began to feel that things, however beautiful, can also be malign. The atmosphere of the Art World reminded me of the morgue. 'All those lovely things passing through your hands,' they'd say – and I'd look at my hands and think of Lady Macbeth. Or people would compliment me on my 'eye,' and my eyes, in rebellion, gave out. After a strenuous bout of New York, I woke one morning half blind. The eye specialist said there was nothing wrong organically. Perhaps I'd been looking too closely at pictures? Perhaps I should try some long horizons? Africa, perhaps? The chairman of Sotheby's said, 'I'm sure there is something wrong with Bruce's eyes but I can't think why he has to go to Africa.'

I went to the Sudan. On camel and foot I trekked through the Red Sea hills and found some unrecorded cave paintings. My nomad guide was a hadendoa, one of Kipling's 'fuzzy-wuzzies'. He carried a sword, a purse and a pot of scented goat's grease for anointing his hair. He made me feel overburdened and inadequate; and by the time I returned to England a mood of fierce iconoclasm had set in.

Not that I turned into a picture slasher. But I did understand why the Prophets banned the worship of images. I quit my job and enrolled as a first-year student of archaeology at Edinburgh University.

My studies in that grim northern city were not a success. I enjoyed a year of Sanskrit. By contrast, archaeology seemed a dismal discipline – a story of technical glories interrupted by catastrophe, whereas the great figures of history were invisible. In the Cairo Museum you could find statues of pharaohs by the million. But where was the face of Moses. One day, while excavating a Bronze-Age burial, I was about to brush the earth off a skeleton, and the old line came back to haunt me:

And curst be he yt moves my bones.

For the second time I quit.

Gradually the idea for a book began to take shape. It was to be a wildly ambitious and intolerant work, a kind of 'Anatomy of Restlessness' that would enlarge on Pascal's dictum about the man sitting quietly in a room. The argument, roughly, was as follows: that in becoming human, man had acquired, together with his straight legs and striding walk, a migratory 'drive' or instinct to walk long distances through the seasons; that this 'drive' was inseparable from his central nervous system; and that, when warped in conditions of settlement, it found outlets in violence, greed, status-seeking or a mania for the new. This would explain why mobile societies such as the gypsies were egalitarian, thing-free and resistant to change; also why, to re-establish the harmony of the First State, all the great teachers – Buddha, Lao-tse, St

Francis – had set the perpetual pilgrimage at the heart of their message and told their disciples, literally, to follow The Way.

The book grew and grew; and as it grew it became less and less intelligible to its author. It even contained a diatribe against the act of writing itself. Finally, when the manuscript was typed, it was so obviously unpublishable that, for the third time, I gave up.

Penniless, depressed, a total failure at the age of thirty-three, I had a phone call from Francis Wyndham of the *Sunday Times* magazine, a man of outstanding literary judgement, whom I hardly knew. Would I, he asked, like a small job as an adviser on the arts? 'Yes,' I said.

We soon forgot about the arts, and under Francis's guidance I took on every kind of article. I wrote about Algerian migrant workers, the couturier Madeleine Vionnet and the Great Wall of China. I interviewed André Malraux on what General de Gaulle thought of England; and in Moscow I visited Nadezhda Mandel-stam.

She lay on her bed, a cigarette stuck to her lower lip, gritting a song of triumph between her blackened teeth. Her work was done. She had published, abroad it was true, but her words would one day come home. She looked at the thrillers I'd been told to take her and sneered: '*Romans policiers!* Next time, bring me some real trash!' But when she saw the pots of orange marmalade, her mouth cracked into a smile: 'Marmalade, my dear, it is my childhood!'

Each time I came back with a story, Francis Wyndham encouraged, criticised, edited and managed to convince me that I should, after all, try my hand at another book. His greatest gift was permission to continue.

One afternoon in the early 70s, in Paris, I went to see the architect and designer Eileen Gray, who at the age of ninety-three thought nothing of a fourteen-hour working day. She lived in the rue Bonaparte, and in her salon hung a map of Patagonia, which she had painted in gouache.

'I've always wanted to go there,' I said. 'So have I,' she added. 'Go there for me.' I went. I cabled the *Sunday Times*: 'Have Gone to Patagonia'. In my rucksack I took Mandelstam's *Journey to Armenia* and Hemingway's *In Our Time*. Six months later I came back with the bones of a book that, this time, did get published. While stringing its sentences together, I thought that telling stories was the only conceivable occupation for a superfluous person such as myself. I am older and a bit stiffer, and I am thinking of settling down. Eileen Gray's map now hangs in my apartment. But the future is tentative.

1983

A PLACE TO HANG
YOUR HAT

Sometime in 1944, my mother and I went by train to see my father aboard his ship, the *Cynthia*, a US minesweeper which had been lent to the British and had docked in Cardiff Harbour for a refit. He was the captain. I was four years old.

Once aboard, I stood in the crow's nest, yelled down the intercom, inspected the engines, ate plum pie in the ward-room; but the place I liked most was my father's cabin – a calm, functional space painted a calm pale grey; the bunk was covered in black oilcloth and, on a shelf, there was a photograph of me.

Afterwards, when he went back to sea, I liked to picture my father in the calm grey cabin, gazing at the waves from under the black-patent peak of his cap. And ever since, the rooms which have really appealed to my imagination have been ships' cabins, log cabins, monks' cells, or – although I have never been to Japan – the tea-house.

Not long ago, after years of being foot-loose, I decided it was time, not to sink roots, but at least to establish a house. I weighed the pros and cons of a whitewashed box on a Greek island, a crofter's cottage, a Left Bank *garçonnière*, and other conventional alternatives. In the end, I concluded, the base might just as well be London. Home, after all, is where your friends are.

I consulted an American – a veteran journalist, who, for fifty years, has treated the world as her back yard.

'Do you really like London?' I asked.

'I don't,' she said, in a gruff and cigarette voice, 'but London's as good as any place to hang your hat.'

That settled it. I went flat-hunting – on my bicycle. I had but five requirements: my room (I was looking for a single room) must be sunny, quiet, anonymous, cheap and, most essentially, within walking distance of the London Library – which, in London, is the centre of my life.

At house agents, I talked to fresh-faced young men who might have had carnations in their buttonholes. They smiled politely when they heard my requirements, and they smiled contempt-uously when they heard how much I had to spend. 'The bed-sitter', they said, 'has vanished from this area of London.'

Beginning my search to the west, I visited a succession of studio conversions, each more lowering than the last, all outrageously priced. I had visions of being ground down by mortgage payments, or by yakking children on the next floor landing. Finally, I explained to a friend of solid Socialist convictions my reasons (which seemed to her perverse) for wanting an attic in Belgravia.

I wanted, I said, to live in one of those canyons of white stucco which belong to the Duke of Westminster and have a faint flavour of the geriatric ward; where English is now a lost language; where, in the summer months, men in long white robes walk the pavements; and where the rooftops bristle with radio antennas to keep the residents in touch with developments in Kuwait or Bahrain.

It was Sunday. My friend glanced down the property columns of the *Sunday Times*; her fingers came to rest beside an entry, and she said, ironically, 'That is your flat.'

The price was right; the address was right; the advertisement said 'quiet' and 'sunny'; but when, on Monday, we went to view it, we were shown a room of irredeemable seediness.

There was a beige fitted carpet pocked with coffee stains. There was a bathroom of black and bilious-green tiles; and there was a contraption in a cupboard, which was the double bed. The house, we were told, was one of two in the street that did *not* belong to the Duke of Westminster.

'Well,' my friend shrugged. 'It's the kind of flat a spy would have.'

It did, however, face south. The ceiling was high. It had a view of white chimneys. There was an Egyptian sheikh on the ground floor; and outside an old black man in a djellabah was sunning himself.

'Perhaps he's a slave?' said my companion.

'Perhaps,' I said. 'Anyway, things are looking up.'

The owner agreed to my offer. I went abroad and learned from my lawyer that the flat was mine.

On moving in, I had to call my predecessor over one or two minor matters – including the behaviour of the phone.

'Yes,' he agreed. 'The phone *is* rather odd. I used to think I was being bugged. In fact, I think the man before me was a spy.'

Now, once you suspect your phone of being bugged, you begin to believe it. And once you believe it, you know for certain that every bleep and buzz on the line is someone listening in. On one occasion, I happened to say the words 'Falkland Islands'; on another, 'Moscow' and 'Novosibirsk' (I was planning a trip on the Trans-Siberian Railway), and, both times, the phone seemed to have an epileptic fit. Or was it my imagination? Obviously it was. For when I changed the old black Bakelite model for something more modern the bleeps and buzzes stopped. I lived for some months in seediness before starting to do the place up.

Very rarely – perhaps never in England – I've gone into a modern room and thought, 'This is what I would have.' I then went into a room designed by a young architect called John Pawson, and knew at once, 'This is what I definitely want.'

Pawson has lived and worked in Japan. He is an enemy of Post-Modernism and other asinine architecture. He knows how wasteful Europeans are of space, and knows how to make simple, harmonious rooms that are a real refuge from the hideousness of contemporary London. I told him I wanted a cross between a cell and a ship's cabin. I wanted my books to be hidden in a corridor, and plenty of cupboards. We calculated we could *just* make a tiny bedroom in place of the green bath. The room, I said, should be painted off-white with wooden Venetian blinds the same colour. Otherwise, I left it to him.

I came back from Africa a few months later to find an airy, well-proportioned room, rather like certain rooms in early Renaissance paintings, small in themselves but with vistas that give an illusion of limitless space. I bought a folding card table to write on, and a tubular chair, which, when not in use, could live out on the landing.

Then I bought a sofa.

Long ago, I used to work for a firm of art auctioneers; and from time to time I still sneak into Sotheby's or Christie's – if only, hypocritically, to congratulate myself on my escape from the 'mania of owning things'. One morning, however, on a trip to the London Library, I looked in on a sale of French furniture at Christie's – and there was no escape.

I saw the kind of sofa you might see in a painting by David. It had rigorous classical proportions and its original pale grey paint. It was stamped by the firm of Jacob-Desmalter and its stretchers were covered with inventory marks from the Château de Versailles – from which one could gather that it had been made for the apartment of the Empress Marie-Louise. Fortunately for me that morning, M. Mitterrand had been elected President of France, and the Paris dealers were not in a buying mood.

Obviously such an object should be upholstered in blue silk damask with gold Napoleonic bees. But the sofa arrived from the upholsterers covered in muslin; and since the chances, either of paying for the damask or of getting it back downstairs, are so remote, the muslin will have to remain.

As for other furniture – although the room needed none – I already had an old French chair, of the Régence, in its original but bashed-up condition. And I had a birchwood table and stool – of the kind my mother used to call 'Swedish Modern'.

I used to see this furniture, sometimes, in the flats of Jewish refugees in Hampstead or Highgate – people who had arrived in London in the late thirties with nothing in their luggage, except their clothes and perhaps a Klee or Kandinsky. It is, of course, designed by Alvar Aalto, and was marketed in London before the war by a firm called Finmar. It was the cheapest modern furniture one could buy: my mother remembers paying five shillings for the stool when she furnished her own one-room flat in 1936.

In my 'art-world' days I was a voracious collector, but only a few pieces remain. Sold the Egyptian relief. Sold the Archaic Greek torso. Sold the fifth-century Attic head. Sold the Giacometti drawing. Sold the Maori carving, which once formed part of Sarah Bernhardt's bed. They were sold to pay for books, or journeys, or simply to eat, during the years of pretending to be a writer.

I cannot regret them. Besides, in my late twenties, I was sick of things; and after travelling some months in the desert, I fell for a kind of 'Islamic' iconoclasm and believed, in all seriousness, that one should never bow before the graven image. As a result, the things that survived this iconoclastic phase are, for the most part, 'abstract'.

I still have, for example, a hanging of blue and yellow parrot feathers, probably made for the back wall of a Peruvian Sun Temple and supposed to date from the fifth century AD. In 1966, I saw a similar piece in the Dumbarton Oaks collection and, on returning to New York, went to see my friend John Wise, who dealt in pre-Columbian art in a room in the Westbury Hotel.

John Wise was a man of enormous presence and a finely developed sense of the ridiculous.

'I'd give anything for one of those,' I said.

'Would you?' he growled. 'How much money have you got in your pockets?'

'I don't know.'

'Empty them, stupid!'

I handed him about $250 – and he handed me back $10 with an equally grumpy 'I suppose you eat lunch.' He then called his assistant to unroll the textile onto the floor.

'Lucky sod!' he called out, as I walked away with it under my arm.

I also have a sheet of Islamic Kufic calligraphy, from the eighth-century Koran – which has a certain talismanic value for a writer, in that Allah first cut a reed pen and with it he wrote the world. There is an Indian painting of a banana tree; a Sienese fifteenth-century cross in tempera and gold; and a gilt-bronze roundel from a Japanese Buddhist temple. Other than that, I have a small collection of Japanese *negoro* lacquers, which once belonged to a German called Ernst Grosse.

Grosse was the Keeper of Japanese Art in the Kaiser-Friedrich Museum in Berlin before the war. Before that, I believe, he lived in the Daitoku-ji in Kyoto. With his friend Eugen Herrigel, the author of *Zen and the Art of Archery*, he was one of the few westerners to appreciate what the Japanese call *wabi*; that is to say 'poverty' in art. My favourite possession is a round box, which surely represents the rising sun, dates from the thirteenth or fourteenth century, and has belonged to a succession of famous tea masters. The story goes that the monks, who made this lacquer, would paint it in a boat moored out on a lake, for fear the dust would spoil the final coat.

Lastly, I have one contemporary sculpture: a fibreglass wall-piece the colour of watermelon, by John Duff. Three times I had gone into houses full of works by famous names; and each time the only work that really grabbed me was by a 'strange man called Duff'. He had once been a surfer and was a student of Zen.

'I have to see this Duff,' I said, and when, finally, I walked into his studio in Chinatown, I knew, for certain, that this was the 'real thing'.

I don't do much writing in my room. For that, I need other conditions and other places. But I can think there, listen to music, read in bed, and take notes. I can feed four friends; and it is, when all is said, a place to hang one's hat.

1984

A TOWER IN TUSCANY

Those of us who presume to write books would appear to fall into two categories: the ones who 'dig in' and the ones who move. There are writers who can only function 'at home', with the right chair, the shelves of dictionaries and encyclopaedias, and now perhaps the word processor. And there are those, like myself, who are paralysed by 'home', for whom home is synonymous with the proverbial writer's block, and who believe naïvely that all would be well if only they were somewhere else. Even among the very great you find the same dichotomy: Flaubert and Tolstoy labouring in their libraries; Zola with a suit of armour alongside his desk; Poe in his cottage; Proust in the cork-lined room. On the other hand, among the 'movers' you have Melville, who was 'undone' by his gentlemanly establishment in Massachusetts, or Hemingway, Gogol or Dostoevsky whose lives, whether from choice or necessity, were a headlong round of hotels and rented rooms – and, in the case of the last, a Siberian prison.

As for myself (for what that's worth), I have tried to write in such places as an African mud hut (with a wet towel tied around my head), an Athonite monastery, a writers' colony, a moorland cottage, even a tent. But whenever the dust storms come, the rainy season sets in, or a pneumatic drill destroys all hope of concentration, I curse myself and ask, 'What am I doing here? Why am I not at the Tower?'

There are, in fact, two towers in my life. Both are mediaeval.

Both have thick walls, which make them warm in winter and cool in summer. Both have views of mountains, contained by very small windows that prevent you from getting distracted. One tower is on the Welsh border, in the water meadows of the River Usk. The other is Beatrice von Rezzori's signalling tower – in her idiomatic English she calls it a 'signallation tower' – built in the days of Guelph and Ghibelline and standing on a hillside of oak and chestnut woods, about twenty-five kilometres east of Florence.

For years I had to admire Beatrice Monti della Corte (as she then was) from afar. She had been a golden girl of the postwar generation on Capri. When she was twenty-three, long before big money clamped its leaden and rapacious hand on the art market, she had opened a gallery in Milan, the Galleria dell'Ariete, one of the first in Europe to show the new New York School of painting. She had bought a sixteenth-century 'captain's house' in Lindos (long before the days of deafening discotheques). Next I heard she had married the Austrian novelist Gregor von Rezzori (or was he Romanian?) and had settled in a Tuscan farmhouse.

One summer evening in England, this couple, whom my imagination had inflated into figures of mythology, were brought to our house. Within minutes we were all old friends: within months I was a regular visitor to Donnini.

The house is a *casa colonica*: the colonists in question being settlers from the Arno Valley who fanned out in waves over the Tuscan countryside from the fourteenth century onwards. Its solid architecture, of stone and tile, is unchanged since that of classical antiquity. Indeed, until about thirty years ago, what Horace had to say of his Tuscan farm could also be said of the life in any *casa colonica*.

At nights the thirty-odd members of an extended family would curl up to sleep under the rafters. By day they would tend their sheep or their beehives, vines and olives. They ploughed the narrow terraced fields with white oxen and lived, austerely, on a diet of bread and beans, cakes of chestnut flour, and meat or pigeon maybe once a month. Then, in the postwar industrial boom, the farmers went to work in the factories, leaving thousands of farms untenanted.

Grisha Rezzori, by temperament and upbringing, is a 'mover': it would be impossible for any biographer to trace his zigzagging course through Europe and America. The Rezzoris were Sicilian noblemen who Austrianised themselves and ended up in the Bukovina, the farthest-flung province of the Austro-Hungarian Empire, now swallowed into the Soviet Union.

A marginal man, cast adrift as a civilian in wartime Germany, he fastened his ironic stare on the fall of the Nazis and its aftermath, and with his prodigious gift for storytelling settled down (more or less!) at Donnini and wove these stories into his monumental novel *The Death of My Brother Abel*.

In summer he would work in a converted hay barn; in winter in a cavernous and book-stacked library where, among his rescued souvenirs, there is a faded sepia photo of the rambling manor, now presumably a collective farm, which was once his family house. Yet to watch Il Barone (as his Tuscan neighbours call him) re-emerging from a snowstorm in a greatcoat after a night walk alone in the woods or to see him strolling through the olive groves with his dogs (or the two tame wild boars Inky and Pinkie) was to realise that he had recovered, or reinvented, the 'lost domain' of his boyhood.

I associate visits to Donnini with hoots of belly laughter. The Rezzoris have a knack of attracting farcical situations. Their immediate neighbours are a well-known German film director and his wife. This couple had friends among the European Far Left. Their guests included Daniel Cohn-Bendit, better known as Danny le Rouge; and somehow the Italian *carabinieri* got it into its collective head that they might be harbouring *Brigate Rosse*. They also got the wrong house and with helicopters and Jeeps staged an 'attack' on the Rezzoris, calling them with loudhailers to come out, unarmed, with their hands up.

The Tower stands a short way from the house on a spur of land overlooking the Arno Valley. When I first went to Donnini, it was lived in by a peasant family and still belonged to the Guicciardini family, whose forebear was the patron of Dante's friend, the poet Guido Cavalcanti. And although Beatrice used to say, with a slightly predatory glint, 'I have a fantasy to buy that Tower,' I confess to having had designs on it myself. As a boy, on a walking tour of Périgord, I had spent hours in Montaigne's famous tower, with the Greek and Latin inscriptions on the rafters, and now I, too, had a fantasy – the fantasy of a compulsive mover – that I would settle down in the smiling Tuscan landscape and take up scholarly pursuits. Beatrice's fantasy, however, was a lot stronger than mine. Besides, I have noticed in her a flair for putting fantasies into action. The tenants left the Tower. She bought it and began the work of restoration. Her friend the Milanese architect Marco Zanuso designed the outside staircase that leads to the upper room. Inside, it became a 'turquerie'; for the Tower of her particular fantasy was another 'lost domain', lying somewhere on the shores of the Bosporus. This part of the story goes back to the mid-20s when Beatrice's father, an aristocrat and expert in heraldry with a great knowledge of history and the fine arts, went to Rome for the winter season and married a fragile Armenian girl who, since the massacres, had been living in Italy.

She died seven years later. Yet the memory of her, of a person unbelievably beautiful and exotic, gave Beatrice an idea to which she has clung all her life: that glamour – real glamour, not the fake Western substitute – is a product of the Ottoman world. Once the rooms of the Tower were plastered, she employed a fresco painter, an old rogue called Barbacci, the last of the locals who could paint a *trompe-l'oeil* cornice or an angel on the ceiling of a church. But when he came to paint the pink 'Ottoman' stripes of the room I write in, he was forever peering from the window at the baronessa in the swimming pool, and some of the stripes have gone awry.

I have never known Beatrice to buy anything but a bargain, even if she has to travel halfway across the world to get it. She bought dhurrie carpets in the Kabul carpet bazaar. Nearer to home, she bought chairs from the Castello di Sammezzano, a fake Moorish palace on a nearby hill. She had, in addition, an assortment of strange objects, of the kind that refugees pack in their trunks: a gilded incense burner; engravings of odalisques; or a portrait of her grandfather, the pasha, who was once Christian governor of Lebanon – objects which needed a home and which, with a bit of imagination, could conjure echoes of lazy summer afternoons in summerhouses by the water.

Whenever I have been in residence, the place becomes a sea of books and papers and unmade beds and clothes thrown this way and that. But the Tower is a place where I have always worked, clearheadedly and well, in winter and summer, by day or night – and the places you work well in are the places you love the most.

1987

GONE TO TIMBUCTOO

Timbuctoo, Tumbuto, Tombouctou, Tumbyktu, Tumbuktu or
Tembuch? It doesn't matter how you spell it. The word is a
slogan, a ritual formula, once heard never forgotten. At eleven I
knew of Timbuctoo as a mysterious city in the heart of Africa
where they ate mice – and served them to visitors. A blurred
photograph, in a traveller's account of Timbuctoo, of a bowl of
muddy broth with little pink feet rising to the surface excited me
greatly. Naturally, I wrote an unprintable limerick about it. The
words 'mice in the stew' rhymed with Timbuctoo and for me
both are still inextricably associated.

There are two Timbuctoos. One is the administrative centre of
the Sixth Region of the Republic of Mali, once French Sudan –
the tired caravan city where the Niger bends into the Sahara, 'the
meeting place of all who travel by camel or canoe', though the
meeting was rarely amicable; the shadeless Timbuctoo that blisters
in the sun, cut off by grey-green waterways for much of the year,
and accessible by river, desert caravan or the Russian airplane that
comes three times a week from Bamako.

And then there is the Timbuctoo of the mind – a mythical city
in a Never-Never Land, an antipodean mirage, a symbol for the
back of beyond or a flat joke. 'He has gone to Timbuctoo,' they
say, meaning 'He is out of his mind' (or drugged); 'He has left his
wife' (or his creditors); 'He has gone away indefinitely and will

27

probably not return'; or 'He can't think of anywhere better to go than Timbuctoo. I thought only American tourists went there.'

'Was it lovely?' asked a friend on my return. No. It is far from lovely; unless you find mud walls crumbling to dust lovely – walls of a spectral grey, as if all the colour has been sucked out by the sun.

To the passing visitor there are only two questions. 'Where is my next drink coming from?' and 'Why am I here at all?' And yet, as I write, I remember the desert wind whipping up the green waters; the thin hard blue of the sky; enormous women rolling round the town in pale indigo cotton *boubous*; the shutters on the houses the same hard blue against mud-grey walls; orange bower-birds that weave their basket nests in feathery acacias; gleaming black gardeners sluicing water from leather skins, lovingly, on rows of blue-green onions; lean aristocratic Touaregs, of super-natural appearance, with coloured leather shields and shining spears, their faces encased in indigo veils, which, like carbon paper, dye their skin a thunder-cloud blue; wild Moors with corkscrew curls; firm-breasted Bela girls of the old slave caste, stripped to the waist, pounding at their mortars and keeping time with monoto-nous tunes; and monumental Songhai ladies with great basket-shaped earrings like those worn by the Queen of Ur over four thousand years ago.

And at night the half-calabash moon reflected in the river of oxidised silver, rippled with the activity of insects; white egrets roosting in the acacias; the thumping of a *tam-tam* in town; the sound of spontaneous laughter welling up like clear water; the bull frogs, whining mosquitoes that prevented sleep, and on the desert side the far-off howls of jackals or the guard-dogs of nomad camps. Perhaps the Timbuctoo of the mind is more potent than one suspects.

It has been claiming European victims, and luring many to their deaths, since it first appeared (as Tembuch) on a Catalan map of the fourteenth century. Rumours had filtered to Europe of an African Kingdom where children of the sun ran about in naked innocence ruled by a wise black monarch called *Rex Melly*. He was often confused with Prester John, the mysterious Christian king who, they prophesied, would rise up out of his country at the head of countless multitudes. He would smite the Infidel, reunite Christendom, and the world would settle down to an everlasting peace. *Rex Melly's* kingdom was also known to the commercially minded as the inexhaustible source of red African gold. Visions of a New Jerusalem beyond the desert were more than tinged with thoughts of commercial enterprise.

But Mansa Mussa, the King of Mali, who gave rise to the legend, was a devout Muslim. Far from smiting the Infidel, the founder of Timbuctoo gave his Arab friends so many golden handshakes on his visit to Cairo in 1324 that the price of gold took a sudden dip on the Cairo exchange. His entourage caused such a stir that a stream of merchants, artisans, scholars and architects, including an Andalucian called Es Saheli, followed him back. A great mosque, and the first black university in the world, rose up from the sand dunes.

The gold of Timbuctoo came from a nearby country. It grew in the ground in nuggets as large as carrots. The men who brought it to market were cannibals and insisted on slave-girls for dinner. But this was a small price to pay in a barter system where gold might be exchanged for its own weight of salt.

By the end of the eighteenth century, Earthly Paradises were in short supply. Most had evaporated under the critical gaze of geographers. The African Association was founded, and was determined that a Britisher should be the first European to set foot in Timbuctoo. And so he did. He did not return. Major Gordon Laing arrived in Timbuctoo in 1826. He wore his uniform throughout, talked grandly of his master, the King of England, and ostentatiously made notes and plans of the city. He was murdered by his escort on leaving the city after refusing conversion to Islam (and probably slavery thereafter).

Two years later the French announced that a Monsieur René Caillié had reached the lost city, dressed as a poor Arab, and returned alive. 'I had formed a totally different idea of the grandeur and wealth of Timbuctoo,' he wrote. 'The city presented, at first sight, nothing but a mass of ill-looking houses, built of earth. Nothing was to be seen in all directions, but immense quicksands of a yellowish white colour ... the most profound silence prevailed.'

The myth of Timbuctoo the Golden had been punctured. Where Chapman could write ...

> *Deep in that lion-haunted inland lies*
> *A mystic city, goal of high enterprise*

the young Tennyson only questioned ...

> *Or is the rumour of thy Timbuctoo*
> *A dream as frail as those of ancient time?*

Apart from the two French forts, the hotel, the lycée and the tactfully hidden quarter for the *colons*, the appearance of Timbuctoo cannot have changed much since Caillié's time. It still presents 'a mass of ill-looking houses, built of earth'. Some, it is true, are built of blocks of white chalk, but the pale alluvial dust works its way into the pores very quickly. Some doorframes are painted a strawberry red incised with green scrolls, the only concession to decoration, and sole legacy of Moroccan conquest.

They still bring in slabs of salt from the dreaded Taodeni mines in the Sahara – a favourite target for anti-slavery societies. The Touareg still prance like storks around the town, on their best behaviour now, for they have little say in the government. They still buy their spears, stone arm bracelets and the indigo veil called the *litham*, for their mouths must never be seen in public. But next door to the Touaregi market booth, a salesman specialises in pots of macaw-coloured brilliantine, black lace brassières, Thermogene Medicated Rub and 'Moon Rabbit Brand Nylon Stockings Made in China'. Such are the changing patterns of trade.

The market women hover over the most unlikely messes. Ochre-coloured calabashes contain a favourite drink – of sour milk, crushed millet and honey. Fricassé of crocodile is also quite common.

The streets are bare and dusty, but if you peer into the courtyards of the richer houses you can see obese women lying on the ground or on low couches. To sit up is thought to ruin the shape of the posterior. Obesity in women is admired, as a symbol of wealth. To maintain such girth in a desiccating desert climate requires mountains of food – all the time. Only the very rich can afford the luxury of a wife so large that she has to be carried by servant girls.

An enthusiastic staff of boys run the hotel for the benefit of the staff. They live like princes. They dress up for dinner and eat sharply at eight. Guests must eat before them or after them. The least request they greet with howls of laughter. They have a communal girlfriend. She is supposed to be the barmaid. More often she can be found on the floor in an agony of laughter. She then has to go home to change. The boys dance most of the night to gramophone records sent from Guinea. They've been dancing here for centuries.

The graffiti are wonderful and worth a special visit to Timbuctoo alone. They range from the simple boy meets boy – '*Mahomet aime Yahya*' – to the overtly political – '*Chinois sont les Cons*'. Happily they are all in neat copybook handwriting and in French.

There are still two bookshops. The Evangelical Library and the

Librairie Populaire du Mali glower at each other across the principal square. Sales cannot be high. Above the Evangelical Library a placard reads '*La Crainte de L'Éternel est le Début de la Sagesse*' – fine words for a people who live sensibly in the Eternal Present. The complete works of Billy Graham are for sale and some postcards.

The Librairie Populaire runs two periodicals – *La Femme Soviétique* and *Les Nouvelles de Moscou*. Newspaper is at a premium, and is very useful for wrapping fish, meat or vegetables in the market. More serious and substantial ideological books, such as the complete works of V. I. Lenin, Mao Tse-Tung, Marx or Engels are allowed to collect dust a little longer before their pages are passed on to the market. They are used for wrapping little packages of dye, chile pepper, snuff, chewing tobacco, the crushed leaves of the baobab tree used as an abortive, or charms to counteract *djinns*. Never throw stones at dogs in Timbuctoo. The lean hounds that skulk in the thorn bushes by day may be the *djinns* that will haunt you by night. A *djinn* starts as a small black spot in the corner of your room and ends up as big as the house. If you believe in *djinns* and the ability of holy men to fly of their own volition, the miracles of the jet age are amateur bungling. 'How long would it take me to fly from here to Mecca?' an old man asked. He might do it in under a day, I told him. He was unimpressed. Local saints regularly take off on a Friday morning and are back the same afternoon. He also knew of a people called the Mericans who claim to have flown to the Moon. 'That is impossible,' he said. 'They are blasphemers.' The inhabitants of Timbuctoo are Arabs, Berbers, Songhoi, Mossi Toucouleur, Bambara, Bela, Malinke, Fulani, Moors and Touaregs. Later came the English, French, Germans, the Russians and then the Chinese. Many others will come and go, and Timbuctoo will remain the same.

1970

II

STORIES

MILK

The young American put his head down to the milk-bowl and the milk darkened, from white to grey, as his head blocked out the light. The bowl was a half calabash. He held it in his palms and felt the warmth coming through. There were black hairs floating on the surface and a faint smell of pitch. He tilted the bowl till the froth brushed against his moustache. 'Shall I?' He paused before his lips touched the milk. Then he tilted it again and gulped.

He drank quickly and with concentration, watching the level sink down the wall of the calabash. The globs of milk cleared his dry, dust-clotted throat. It was stronger than milk in America and left a bitter taste on the tongue.

'Be careful what you eat, Jeb.' The voice was sharp and pleading. 'And don't, whatever you do, touch the milk. The milk's tainted in them countries.'

In his mind Jeb Andrews saw the careful white clapboard house and the drawn face of his mother.

'I know you'll be all right, Jeb. But that shan't keep me from worryin'. If you was goin' to Europe, I shouldn't be worryin', but Africa, Jeb, and them blacks.'

He drained the bowl and turned it over. White drops splashed on his rawhide boots, now red with dust. The outside of the calabash was a warm golden colour and the surface scratched with drawings of animals and plants. It had broken in two places, but the woman had sewn it up with tarred twine. That was what gave off the pitchy smell. Jeb Andrews thought the calabash a lovely thing.

It was mid-day and the sky was hazy and white hot. Sweat streamed inside his shirtfront and down the small of his back. The blood ran into his feet and they felt as if they'd burst his boots.

The women were Peuls. They sold milk to bus travellers under the speckled shade of an acacia. It was the one shade tree for miles. They were lean and angular, as nomad women are. They wore shifts of indigo cotton and the blue rubbed off on their glistening brown skin. Big brass rings weighted their earlobes down.

'Another,' Jeb said to the woman.

He felt for a coin in his damp pocket. The woman set the bowl in the dust and ladled it full. A baby sucked at her nipple, its pink fingers clawing at her breast. Jeb watched a dribble of milk run from the corner of the baby's mouth.

The woman grabbed the coin and tied it in a knot of cotton. She flashed her teeth and then hid them. Her companions looked on, amused and disdainful, gaping at the thin boy in the dusty whites, his golden hair spilling round the half sphere of the calabash.

'Like it's feeding time at the zoo,' Jeb thought. 'Like I'm the animal.'

'And another thing, Mr Andrews, I advise you not to drink unboiled milk. The French veterinarians have reported outbreaks of brucellosis all along the northern zone.'

Jeb could hear again the flat voice of the Peace Corps doctor and see the disapproving lips and untanned face above a spotless overall. The doctor had given him sterilising tablets and packets of dehydrated food. He had not used them. Jeb drank the milk in spite of and because of the doctor.

Set apart from the others was a small shrunken woman, her legs reduced to spindles, her lips cracked, her hair scabbed and matted and her breasts shrivelled to leathery purses. She crouched with her sex uncovered, not caring, or shuffled round the women, picking up pieces of old calabash. Jeb watched her arrange them in piles as if, by fitting them together, she could repair her broken womb.

He had been three weeks on the road. The strangeness of Africa had worn off and somehow, in the heat and light, Africa was less unbelieveable than home. It was winter in Vermont. He tried to picture it, but the picture kept slipping from focus, leaving only the heat and light.

Still, he worried about Old Herb. In the fall they'd stood on the bridge below the store. They'd been lumbering all day and the leaves fell, red over yellow, into the river.

'Sad you're goin',' Herb had said. 'Shan't last the winter through. That's how I'm feelin' anyways.'

'I'll be back, Herb.'

'Don't mind me, Jeb. You got to go. And don't mind your mother none. You can't sit back home with her fussin' you. You're grown enough to know your mind.' There was a lump in his throat. The snow would be piled up round Herb's cabin and it troubled him to think of it.

Jeb Andrews found his body thinning and hardening all the time, and the old prejudices stripping away. The Africans fascinated him – the mammas, the big cheerful grain-filled mammas; and the Hausa men, their faces scarred like cat whiskers and their shiny skins reflecting the blue of their clothes and the blue of the sky so it was the colour of night without a trace of brown; and the Peul boys strutting about with swords and black leather kilts and ostrich feathers in their hats. Jeb was beginning to feel how they looked. He even learned to spit like an African 'Yiakchh … ptoo …' and the ball of saliva would roll in the dust and disappear.

He loved the smell of fresh-flailed millet in the villages and the bulging mud granaries and rhythmic thumping of pestles; the termitaries splashed white by vultures and the red laterite road streaking through the thorn savannah. The bark of the bushes was orange or pale green and their spines were long and white as icicles. In the heat of the day the Peuls' cattle roamed among them. They had rippling brown coats and white lyre-shaped horns. Jeb thought them the loveliest animals in the world. He did not believe their milk could be diseased.

The driver called the passengers back to the bus. The road forked north away from the river. The earth became less red and the baobab trees fatter and more stunted. They reached the town late in the afternoon and stopped outside a bar called Le Lotus Bleu. A mad boy was whirling in the street. In the bar-room some Africans were drinking. Jeb ordered a beer from the owner, a squat Vietnamese woman with her head in a flowered scarf. A man came in selling meat on a metal tray. She prodded it with her pudgy fingers.

'The meat's too tough,' she said.

The Africans laughed.

'You be the one that's tough, Mamma, not this meat.'

The old woman liked being teased and squealed with pleasure. Jeb compared her happy face with Vietnamese women in magazines.

'Have you a room?' he asked.

'This is a bar,' she said, 'not a *bordel*.' And the men laughed again. 'For a bed you must go to the *campement*. There is a white woman in the *campement*.'

Jeb walked between mud walls to the edge of town, and then up an alley of acacias, now black and leafless in the dry season. On a hill was a low whitewashed building with rounded arches. Once it had been the legionaires' mess. There was a tennis court, now cracked and pitted, with the net frayed off. The white woman was hanging her laundry on the wire. She had red hair out of a bottle and her eyelids were painted black and green. Her skin hung loosely in a collar round the base of her neck. Jeb thought she looked a bit like a goldfish.

'Madame Annie?'

'Oui.' She stared coldly, without surprise or welcome.

'Est-ce que vous avez une chambre?' he said slowly.

'I have a room,' she replied in English. 'Come this way please.'

Under the arches were metal chairs and tables covered in green plastic. He followed her into the courtyard where there was an aviary with doves and a caged monkey. Some bougainvillaea straggled over a trellis. She called, 'Osman. Key for number five,' and an old Touareg shuffled over. She unlocked a green door. The room was bare but for a cot bed and tattered mosquito net hanging from the ceiling. The whitewash was peeling and there were pale geckos on the walls.

'A thousand francs a day,' she said. 'Service included.'

'Have you anything cheaper?'

'The cheapest,' she said unhelpfully.

The room was expensive but he was tired and took it. He had slept three nights by the roadside.

Jeb stripped. He stepped out of his pants and left them in a heap on the floor. The red dust had caked on his skin. He lay naked on the bed. A cooler wind came in off the desert and through the shutters. He felt the sweat drying on his parts.

It was dark when he woke. He dressed and walked under the arches to the pissoir. Passing Madame Annie's room he heard creaking springs and the sighs and whimperings of love. The blind was not fully drawn and he caught sight of a sinuous black body laid over a pile of pink flesh.

He washed and went out onto the terrace. Insects were whining round a single electric bulb. Another white woman sat drinking. She was very thin and tragic-looking. Her blonde hair hung in rat-tails, and her face was lopsided from a broken jaw. One arm was in a sling. The monkey had bitten her hand.

'The Madame is sleeping,' she said.

'Not sleeping exactly,' Jeb said.

'Is disgusting,' she said. 'She makes love with Africans so they will not call her racist. Her husband leave her when she go with Africans. Now I think she hates white men.'

The woman's name was Gerda. She came from Alsace and was stranded without money. Once she had worked as a journalist and had exposed French atrocities in the Algerian War. She had great sympathy for Arabs and great hatred for blacks and Jews. She said France was overrun by Jews. Even de Gaulle was a Jew. Jeb knew about anti-Semitism but he had not heard the words 'pestilence', 'bacillus', 'infection' and 'cancer' used for people.

She said Madame Annie treated her as a servant. She got no reply to her letters for help. She had called the postmaster a dirty drunk and he had called her a Nazi Imperialist. She suspected him of burning her mail.

The door of Annie's room opened and a boy in bright blue jeans trod limberly across the yard. He nodded to Madame Gerda who ignored him.

'Is disgusting,' she said.

Madame Annie followed the boy out, composed and un-dishevelled in a tartan skirt. She asked Jeb if he wanted dinner and called to Osman to roast a pintade. Madame Gerda sat pretending to read a newspaper.

The pintade was tough and the Algerian wine went to Jeb's head. Later some of Annie's regulars came up to drink her whisky. It was the only whisky in town. There were several Africans in European dress and an ex-legionnaire, a small, heat-wrinkled man with grey hair *en brosse*.

The whore who lived in the *campement* heard the noise and came out to join the party.

'Mamzelle Dela,' the legionnaire greeted her. 'La Belle de la Brousse!'

She was a Peul. She had a Peul woman's wonderful high cheekbones and chiselled lips, and long straight gleaming legs and a short body flexible as a hinge. She wore a tight pink dress in one piece. She put her elbows on the table and gazed in Jeb's direction. He felt her huge black eyes undressing him.

The men sang a song with a refrain ending 'Annie et son whisky!' and Annie began a discussion on whether Adam forced the apple on Eve or Eve prostituted herself for the apple.

'Why don't you drink?' the legionnaire called across. 'What are you, some kind of Englishman?'

'I'm an American.'

'Ha! Ha! L'Équipe CIA! Boom! Boom! Come and drink some whisky. Annie, give this young spy some whisky.'

'I don't drink whisky,' Jeb said.

'You must drink whisky,' Annie said. 'For the bacterias. Whisky massacres bacterias. Osman.'

'Madame.'

'Whisky for the young man.'

'A very small one,' said Jeb.

'You pour what you like. Osman does not like to pour whisky. He is a Mussulman and he hates the drink. One day I give him pastis for his throat and he is drunk. I do not think he forgives me.'

Osman fetched the bottle, holding it gingerly as a bomb. He passed it to Jeb, who poured out half an inch.

'More,' said Annie. 'More.'

She took the bottle and filled the glass over half. She kept her own Johnny Walker beside her on the table. She gave herself another and marked the level with a pencil.

'I cannot live without whisky,' she said.

'It's tea,' whispered Mamzelle Dela darkly. Jeb was troubled and excited when she looked at him.

'This hotel is not my métier,' said Madame Annie. 'Soon I shall retire to the bush. I shall take a pretty black boy. I shall build a hut and sell my jewels to pay for the whisky. Some people die in a convent and I shall die in the bush.'

Jeb agreed it was better than a convent.

'I have seen many jungles,' she said, 'and the worst jungle is a convent. Very unhealthy place. In a convent people hate each other all the time. In the jungle they hate each other sometimes but not always.'

'Mon Dieu, que ce garçon est beau,' said Mamzelle Dela.

'She says you are a beautiful boy.'

'She's pretty nice herself.'

'Et il est américain?'

'American.'

'Je l'adore.'

'She says she loves you.'

'I love her too.'

'You never say you was American,' said Annie.

'I thought you knew.'

'I think you was English. Very hypocrite people, English. I was many times in England, in the war, after the war. Terrible! Once I was in English city. The name of this place is Hull. I am coming from Germany with my German lover. We go to a boarding house and the woman is so nice and polite and say how much she likes the Germans, which is not at all true because English hate Germans. She thinks we are Germans both, and she shows the room. Nice room. All flowers à la manière anglaise. Then she says with a charming, really a charming smile, "Of course you are married?" And I say, "Mais non, Madame. Certainement pas!" and this woman, which is smiling, is now smiling not, but screaming, "Out of my house. This is a nice house. You have not business here. Go to the bordel where you belong."'

'I never went to England,' Jeb said.

'I tell you, my God, they are very hypocrite.'

'I heard that.'

'They are dirty and they think they are clean. Hull is bad, my dear, but Londres is worse than Hull. This German man and me, we go to a film. Un film cochon. I don't speak lies. Old people naked. Gens de soixante ans tous nus. Doing things you can't imagine. Then they invite us to sing a hymn to the Queen. And in Hyde Park, my God, under the trees! Feet, my God! Que des pieds!'

The men fed the juke-box and played Togolese rock. The legionnaire stumbled to his feet and dragged Mamzelle Dela by the arm and tried to dance. She put on a long-suffering look and winked at Jeb.

He winked back.

'You have loved an Africaine?' asked Annie.

'Never,' Jeb said in an even voice. He had never been to bed with a woman, but he did not want to show this.

'You must go with Mamzelle Dela. She wants it.'

Jeb turned red and felt his self-confidence running away.

'Listen,' she said protectively. 'I speak with you as a mother. You are afraid to go with her because you have heard bad things. I tell you, African women are cleaner than white women. They are très pudique. And they are much more beautiful.'

'You think I should?'

'I know it.'

The legionnaire was too drunk to dance and stood with his arms round her buttocks. His head nuzzled her breasts, but he was slipping gradually to the floor.

'Down,' he spluttered. 'Down … down … down … down …'

'Down where?'

'Down into the cave.'

'Monsieur, you know very well the price of entry is five thousand francs.'

'Ah! Dela. Black, beautiful and cruel.'

Now he was sitting crouched and trying to get a hand up her legs. Dela clamped them tight. She winked again.

'Black, beautiful and cruel.'

'C'est un con,' she said definitely.

Jeb helped get the legionnaire back to his chair. There Dela pulled him and they were dancing. He loosened up and his legs flew. Then they closed and her hard belly burned through his pants, and he was pumped hard, and there were hot shivers up his back. Then they were in her room, he standing and she sitting on the bed, her quick fingers unzippering, and he praying, thinking of nothing and nobody else now, but praying it would come right. And then they were on the bed and clinching, and then she pushed him away and sat up.

'I need a sandwich,' she said. 'You pay my sandwich.'

'Oh! No. God. Not now.'

'You pay my sandwich.'

'I pay your sandwich.'

'You pay my beer.'

'I pay also your beer.'

He got up and took a note from his pocket. She put on a blue boubou and stalked out into the kitchen. She was back in five minutes munching a chicken sandwich and smacking her lips. Then she tied her hair in a bandana and was ready.

But Jeb was face down on the pillow, his head spinning from the whisky. She lay beside him and her hand felt him soft and limp.

'Pederast,' she snorted.

'No. No.' Jeb hit the pillow miserably. 'No. No.'

'All Americans are pederasts.'

She rolled over and began to snore, and her snores did not keep him from sleeping.

But in the morning it was different. From that morning he would never forget the white light and blowing curtains, and never stop thanking for the taut breasts; the hard mouth freely given; the powerful arms; the nails that raised red welts on his back; the soles of her feet sandpapering his thighs; again and again, two bodies floating and then heavy along the uneven line where the brown met white; and afterwards, when they were both tired together, her amused smile and her fingers gently disentangling his hair. He left her and walked across the terrace. Madame Gerda turned her face to the wall. Madame Annie was knitting a pink jumper. She looked over her spectacles and smiled.

'You are even walking differently,' she said.

1977

THE ATTRACTIONS OF FRANCE

THE JOURNEY UP

The men waited for the truck in a tight rectangle of shade under the blue wall. The sun was glaring bright and sucked the colour from the dusty red street. The men were squatting. They had pulled their blue cottons above their knees. Their legs were lean and brown and the soles of their feet were rough as sandpaper.

A boy was walking up the shadow of the wall scuffing the dust with his feet. His hair was red but it was the caked dust that coloured it. He put down a kitbag and sat by me.

'You are going to Atar?'

'You too?'

'I am going to France.'

He was short and stocky, perhaps twenty. His hard thighs bulged through white jeans that were now ruddy pink from the dust. He had not washed for some time. He smelled strong and acrid though the smell was not objectionable. He had been chewing cola nuts and they had dyed his gums orange. His thin curling mouth showed off his Moorish blood. The Moors ignored him. He was very black.

'What will you do in France?'

'Continue my profession.'

'What's that?'

'*Installation sanitaire.*'

'You have a passport?

'No I need one not. I am a sailor. I have a sailor's paper.'

He squeezed his hand in his back pocket and with two fingers fished for a scrap of damp and crumpled paper.

The writing was in Spanish: 'I, Don Hernando Ordoñez, certify that Patrice Diolé has worked as Seaman Third Class ...'

'From Atar,' he said, 'I will go to Villa Cissneros. I will take a ship to Gran Canaria. I will go to France, to Yugoslavia, to China, and continue my profession.'

'As sanitary engineer?'

'No, Monsieur. As adventurer. I will see all the peoples and all the countries of the world.'

The truck came, almost filled up with sacks of sorghum and rice. The Senegalese and Moors climbed aboard. We followed. The trip to Atar was a bad trip, dust storm all the way. The Moors pulled down the folds of their blue turbans, covering their faces and leaving the narrowest horizontal strip through which their eyes glittered. The Senegalese wore a variety of head gear. One man wore his underpants. His nose, not his eyes, showed through the vertical slit.

The truck stopped at a police post. A gendarme climbed up and counted fifty-nine bodies lying in among the sacks. The law prohibited more than thirty. The gendarme was a Sarakolle from the river. He was not making his people move. The Moors were in their country now and they weren't moving either. All fifty-nine went on into the dust and the night.

I had been squeezed against the sanitary engineer for twelve hours. 'Tell me,' he said. 'Have you seen the Indians?'

'Yes.'

'It's a village or what?'

'It's a big country with too many people. You should go see it.'

'*Tiens*. I always thought it was a village.'

AT THE MINE

From the hill we looked down over the flat country, golden white and spotted black with flat-topped thorn trees; you could see why they once called it 'leopard country'. Below us was the mine. There were grey spoil tips and the new American crushing plant, green with purple scaffolding, and the old French mine that went bust, because the copper was low-grade ore and they couldn't ship it out economically. There were silver fuel tanks and shiny aluminium cabins and yellow cranes and bulldozers. Beyond we could see the town of mudbrick boxes, and shanties made of packing cases, and the tents of the nomads.

The Major pointed to a grey hill where he had shot gazelles.

'Nice view,' he said. 'Thought you'd like it up here.' He looked at his watch.

'Sorry, I'm afraid we have to go. I'm on parade at lunch. You'll see.'

The Major was a neat, sandy-haired man, greying at the temples. He wore khaki shorts, had a red face and red knees, and smiled with a humorous grin. He had been retired from the British Army and was working as personnel manager for the mine. The company was American, but the Government did not allow Americans to staff it, because of Israel. Most of the mining engineers were French. The Major had the unenviable job of keeping Frenchmen happy in the desert and keeping American shareholders happy by keeping the costs down.

'Let me blind you with a statistic,' he said. We were taking our trays in the canteen. 'It costs six times less to keep an Englishman in the desert than a Frenchman, and three times less than a Yank.'

We helped ourselves to *artichaut vinaigrette* and *filet de boeuf* with mushrooms and a carafe of *beaujolais nouveau*. The month was December. There were Frenchmen eating at most tables. The Major and I both wore khaki shorts. The Frenchmen stared at our knees and raised their eyebrows, nodding.

48

'The English like filthy food,' I said.

'Probably something to do with the war,' said the Major.

'Probably.'

'I mean, Englishmen have had to make do.'

'Not all of them,' I said.

I had been eating goat and couscous for some days.

'It's delicious,' I said.

'You wait,' the Major said. 'They'll soon come over and complain.'

'There's nothing to complain about.'

'They'll find something. If we got the *Tour d'Argent* to fly their meals out, they'd still complain.'

'Only tourists go to the *Tour d'Argent*.'

'You get in Vichy and they want Evian. You get Evian and they want Perrier. Can't win. I suggested a complaints book so they could air specific grievances. They weren't having it. Want to complain personally. It's supposed to be a safety valve.'

'Rough on you,' I said.

'Can't get used to being a safety valve for French steam.'

'It must be hard.'

'I should put in for a change.'

By working abroad and avoiding the taxman, the Major was hoping to set aside a small capital sum to retire on. His wife had been out here. She had sat in the cabin with gardening catalogues. Planning her garden had kept her sane, but she couldn't take the heat.

The Major and I ate the main course. Then a big man in blue jeans came over. He had a lock of black hair rat-tailing down his forehead. He held out his Camembert on a plate.

'Monsieur, ce Camembert n'est pas mur.'

'What's he say?'

'It's not ripe.'

'It's cheese not fruit.'

'C'est dur.'

'It's hard.'

'I could tell him where to stuff it but I won't.'

'On ne met pas les bons fromages dans le frigo.'

'You shouldn't put good cheese in the icebox.'

'We took 'em out last week,' the Major said, 'and they went orange.'

The man shrugged and went back to his table. He showed the Camembert to his friends and squeezed it with his thumb.

'We'll never understand the Frogs,' said the Major. 'Niggers are much less foreign to me than Frogs. I've lived with niggers all my life. Bright, some of 'em. Really bright.'

'Very bright,' I said.

'Not like the Moors. Gimme a nigger any day over a Moor. Less stuck on religion.'

'Much less stuck.'

'You can work with niggers, but the Moors give an awful lot of bother.'

'How's that, Major?'

'They won't work and they don't want anyone else to work. Government owns half this mine and doesn't even want it to pay.'

'Perhaps it's something to do with their religion.'

'Bloody religion.'

'I read somewhere that Moors believe copper's the property of the Devil.'

'It is the property of the Devil. I could have told you that. All mining engineers are Devils. For sheer arrogance they beat the lot. Think they can blast through anywhere.'

'They are tough,' I said.

'You know something?' The Major returned to the Moors. 'Moors remind me of Frogs. Same look. Both look at you as though you're dirt.'

'Don't let them get you down.'

'But I hate 'em. We had a welder here. A Belgian. Good boy. I used to cut his hair. Fell fifteen feet and broke his neck on a girder. And the Moor who was helping him stood by and laughed. Laughed! Stood there laughing. It makes you sick.'

In the evening it was windy and flights of swifts cut the green air. It was the third year of the drought. The nomads had lost most of their livestock and flocked to the fringes of the mining camp.

In the market a marabout was reciting the suras of the Koran. He was blind. His eyes were almonds of red veins and cloudy blue-white cataracts. His words came harsh and soaring as a drum solo. An old man kept time with one hand. He rested the other hand on the marabout's shoulders. He was his father.

Some camel men were saddling up. The saddles were of red and yellow leather. The men hated the mine.

The Major hoped to get me a ride down on the company plane. He said we shouldn't know until the last minute. He telephoned and got word that a Frenchman had cancelled.

'Cheers!' he called. 'You've a seat.'

We drove to the airstrip but found another Frenchman who had taken his friend's place. So we drove back into town and found a white pick-up ready to leave. They were waiting for one more passenger. I squeezed in behind the tailboard.

'I'm awfully sorry about the plane,' the Major said.

'Don't think about it.'

'You look pretty uncomfortable.'

'But will survive.'

'It does seem awful after promising the plane.'

'I said not to worry, Major.'

'It's a shame. Bloody Frogs.'

'Don't let them get you down.'

'Easier said than done. No fun stuck in the desert with a lot of Frogs.'

The engine started and the red rear light lit up the Major's shorts and knees.

'We're off,' I said. 'Goodbye, Major, and thanks.'

'Cheers!' said the Major, looking miserable.

THE JOURNEY BACK

The boy lay on the floor of the pick-up. His long tapering hands held onto a cotton sheet. He was trying to keep the dust off his clothes. They were beautiful clothes, green pants, a yellow sweater and a scarf striped orange and white. He had worn them fresh to start the journey and now they were greasy and floury with sand.

He was the best-looking boy I ever saw. He had the kind of looks to make anyone feel ugly and inadequate. He was frightened and unhappy and kept rolling his huge black eyes and shivering.

'Where are you going?'

'Dakar.'

'Home?'

'They turned me back at the frontier. I had a passport and they turned me back.'

He was all broken up about being turned back.

'Where were you going?'

'Paris.'

'To study?'

'To continue my profession.'

'What's that?'

'You wouldn't understand.'

'I would.'

'Non, Monsieur. Comprenez–pas. C'est un métier special.'

'I know most occupations in France.'

'But this métier, no.'

'Say it.'

'You will not understand. I am an ébéniste. I make *bureaux-plats*, Louis Quinze and Louis Seize.'

THE ESTATE OF
MAXIMILIAN TOD

On 6 February 1975, Dr Estelle Neumann fell down a crevasse of the Belgrano Glacier in Chilean Patagonia.

Her death robbed Harvard University of the finest glaciologist at work in the United States; I lost a close ally and a good friend. I cannot think of Estelle without recalling her humour, her capacity for statistics and the blind, unreflecting courage that lacked the imagination to turn round.

Her work has continued, but in lesser hands; I could say treacherous hands. In February of last year, her research student Dr (now Professor) Helmut Leander, of the Institute of Glacial Studies at Kydd College, Minnesota, published a 103-page attack on her *Glaciers of the Southern Hemisphere*. Then in September, at the Symposium of World Climatology in Tel-Aviv, he described her findings as 'irresponsible'. That evening, in the bar of the Hilton Hotel, I overheard shreds of his conversation explaining, in German and to an audience of West Germans, how the Neumann Theory was the product of its author's incurable optimism. 'Or else,' he added in a whisper, 'she was bought.'

I checked her figures. I double-checked them. The work took me six weeks: it left me red-eyed and exhausted. Estelle had scribbled her material over thirteen hip-pocket notebooks with black leatherette covers – equations, graphs and diagrams, which she alone could decipher, or someone as close to her as I. I was obliged to do it, as much for her memory as to reassure the organisations that had invested in our research. I found no fault with her data, her method or her conclusions.

Estelle's work was bound to upset the catastrophists. She had proved beyond question that the injection of fossil fuels into the atmosphere had no effect whatever on the temperature of glaciers. The prospects of triggering off another Ice Age, at least within the next 10,000 years, were nil. And the pronouncements of Dr Leander and his colleagues merely reflected that bias for self-destruction now engrained in American academic circles. 'Those dodos!' she would sigh. 'Those dodos!'

Estelle published her thesis in 1965 and from that year her work attracted the attention of the chemical, the petrochemical and aerospace industries. The Cliffhart Foundation (a subsidiary of Heartland Oil) financed our first project to the tune of $150,000. For five months we studied the structure of Tyndall Flowers, the six-petalled cavities which appear in parallel layers on the surface of melting ice and resemble the superimposed calligraphies of some Japanese Zen Master. (The other expert in the field, Dr Nonomura Hideyoshi, had retired to a monastery near Nara.)

Before we had finished, nineteen other foundations pressed us to accept whatever money we needed. No expense seemed unreasonable to their trustees: they only wished the work to continue.

On 9 October 1974, a luminous fall day whirling with scarlet leaves, Estelle and I lunched at the Harvard Faculty Club to discuss our expedition to the Belgrano ice-cap. Our Eggs Benedict were all but uneatable, our conversation drowned by the braying accents of five Oxford historians at the next table.

Estelle was forty-three, a handsome, masculine woman with black hair cropped short and worn in a fringe above her considerable eyebrows. Years of exposure to sun, wind and snow had burnished her skin the texture of shoe-leather; when not beaming with self-satisfaction, her crow's-feet showed up white.

Her dress was simple and unaffected, a sweater and tweed skirt for the laboratory, hardly anything more elaborate for the cheese-fondue parties she gave in her Cambridge apartment. But she was addicted to 'primitive' jewellery of the worst kind – Navajo turquoise, African bangles, amber beads. That morning a golden eagle of the Veraguas Culture was flapping between her breasts; I did not have the heart to tell her it was a fake.

Over lunch Estelle gave me a critical résumé of the literature on Patagonian glaciers. She could remember if a pamphlet was printed in Valdivia or Valparaiso in 1897 or 1899. She drew my attention to some new work by Dr Andrei Shirokogoff, of the Antarctic Institute in Novosibirsk, who explored the north face of Cordon Tannhäuser during the Allende years. But her conversation kept harping back to certain topographical details of the Belgrano Glacier.

She eyed me in a peculiar way. She asked a number of penetrating questions about our research fund – which was most unlike her. She even asked questions about our Swiss accounts. I can safely say that my face was a total blank until she gave up and reverted to her superior manner. She then spoke of Vaino Mustanoja's *Patagonian Researches*, published in English, in Helsinki, in 1939.

'You'll love old Mustanoja,' she said. 'His prose style is simply entrancing.'

Now Estelle knew nothing about prose style and her choice of the word 'entrancing' lay far outside her usual range of adjectives.

'I've got to have it photostatted,' she went on. 'I promised old Shirokogoff a copy. Know something? Peabody's got the only copy in existence. Think! The Finns don't even have a copy.'

Excusing myself, I hurried to the library of the Peabody Museum and withdrew the quarto volume whose existence I had overlooked. The pink paper cover was charmingly illustrated with Mustanoja's own copper plate engraving of the Belgrano. Rustic letters, of nothofagus twigs, formed the titles. Around the borders were vignettes of the ethnographical specimens he collected from the Tehuelche Indians on his 1934 expedition and presented to the Rovaniemi Museum.

It touched me to think of these southerly artefacts in that northernmost city. I turned to pp. 141–2. The stroke of a razor, two neat folds and the sheet was in my pocket. Mustanoja's prose style, it so happens, is outstanding for a Finn:

From Lago Angostura the track led across a plain denuded by wind erosion and sparsely covered with xerophytic plants. Stunted bushes of calafate (*Berberis Darwinii*) managed to exist, but the region was wild and poor, deserted by guanacos, unsuitable for sheep. After marching twenty-three miles with dust from the salt-pans streaming into my eyes, the wooded valley of the Rio Tannhäuser came into view. Beyond, I could see the pink and green strata of the Meseta Colorado; beyond that, the azure ice-caps of the Andean Cordillera.

A descent of two hours brought me into the logging camp of Puesto Ibáñez, where I had hoped to purchase a meal from the inhabitants. For a week my diet had been reduced to grilled military starlings (*Trupialis militaris*), which were by no means easy to shoot, having exceptionally hard crania for birds of their size.

The settlement, however, was in ruins, thanks to the activities of a Chilean bandit. A woman squatted before the charred remains of her cottage, holding a dead baby and pointing with an expression of abject misery at the half-dug grave of her husband.

This dismal scene was offset, somewhat, by a magnificent *Embothrium coccineum* ablaze with scarlet flowers. Along the riverbank were groves of fuchsia (*F. Magellanica*), bamboos (*Chusquea Cumingia*) and of *Saxegothaea conspicua*. An alstromeria was in bloom, as were yellow violets, calceolarias, the snowdrop orchis and an orange mimulus, which proved to be a new species and which my friend, Dr Bjorn Topelius of Uppsala, has named *M. Mustanojensis* in my honour.

Three miles upstream I came on a burnt timber shack, fresh evidence of the bandit's work, from which I removed an interesting human calvarium. I pitched camp on an inviting meadow where, to my satisfaction, I noticed the fresh spoor of some Huemul deer and walked off to shoot my dinner.

I had not gone three hundred yards when a doe came into my sights: I dispatched her with a single shot. A fawn then rushed up to its dead mother: I dispatched it as well. I had not, however, noticed that the buck had come within range of the fawn. My second shot passed through the skull of the latter and carried away the symphysial region of the lower jaw of the former. I was thus obliged to kill the third animal and exterminate the family.

In the morning, thoroughly nourished, I set off to explore the Meseta Colorado ...

The next page of *Patagonian Researches* – and even now I tremble at the thought of revealing its contents – describes Mustanoja's discovery of a 'lost' valley overlooked by the British surveyors of the Holditch Commission in 1902. It appalled me to think that Estelle was aware of its existence.

On 3 November I flew from New York to Buenos Aires. I was alone, having arranged for her to give the F.Z. Boeing Memorial Lecture in Seattle, an invitation she could hardly refuse. We agreed to meet in January at a point on the Argentine frontier near Esquel.

I reached Lago Angostura on 9 November. The settlement had

grown since Mustanoja's time. The estancia now belonged to a German, Don Guillermo Meingast, who came here after World War II. There was a police post, a gas-pump and the Hotel-Bar Alhambra, a corrugated iron building, painted a livid green but stripped by salt dust on the windward side.

The owner was a sorrowful young widow running to fat who spent her days lacquering her nails and leafing through Argentine football magazines. Dinner, the invariable dinner of the Patagonian pampas, consisted of a can of sardines, a lump of lamb that bounced on the plate and acid red wine that came in a penguin jug.

The two other customers wore hard hats and sat by a window playing dominoes. One was a big weatherbeaten man with an implacable mouth and wandering eyes, dressed from head to foot in black. His partner was a hunchback Indian dwarf.

The dwarf won the game and said, 'Vamos!' quietly, and the big man sheathed his knife and sat him on his forearm. Together they rode off into the storm.

The track to Puesto Ibáñez still answered Mustanoja's description, but there was no sign of the logging camp and the valley floor was choked with bamboos. No traveller without a copy of *Patagonian Researches* could have found his way up the cliffs of the Meseta.

At 5,050 feet – if my aneroid reading is correct – I stood on Chilean territory and looked down from the ridge where Mustanoja first sighted the valley. I let my eyes wander over the sights he described so vividly: the barrage of purple clouds ringing the ice-caps; the 'hole' of clear blue sky; the rainbows; the chutes of light rain; the Belgrano itself 'streaming like the folds of a wedding garment': the glittering screes of micaceous schist, the black forests and, far below, the river snaking through bright green pastures.

More than ever I realised what he meant by 'the ideal

microclimate'. I followed the track downwards, zigzagging through a 'flowering mead' of columbines, tulips, narcissi, widow iris, crocuses and fritillaries – all Asiatic species; in fact, the number of rarities from the Caucasus and Hindu Kush made it clear that the plantsman was a botanist of no ordinary competence. I stopped beside a gnarled cypress to rest in a hut built of bark and tree roots and modelled on Rousseau's hermitage in the park at Ermenonville (after the engraving by Hubert Robert). And the track itself was no less a work of art – spread with white gravel and so graded to ensure perfect footfalls with all debris and jarring stones removed.

Brushing through curtains of jade-green lichen I plunged into the dark wood of *Nothofagus antarctica*, silent but for the toc-tocking of Magellan woodpeckers. Another descent of 1,000 feet brought me into the dappled sunlight of young specimen trees – poplars, paulownias, wing-nuts, Siberian birches and the blue-needled Kurile larch.

The valley floor was an expanse of undulating turf that proved not to be of grass, but a carpet of the prostrate Andean strawberry, studded with fruit that gave off a delicious smell when crushed.

A cobalt ribbon of *Iris Kaempferi* bordered a lake whose waters were the palest silvery celadon and so transparent that the trout floating over its bed of white stones seemed to be airborne.

These irises were the only blue flowers in the valley. Otherwise, the vegetation consisted of white willows, white-margined aralias, silver whitebeams and the tansy-leaved thorn. Among the flowers were a white eremurus, Moutan peonies, the Mount Omei rose and the waxy pagodas of the giant Himalayan lily. Or else the plants were black, black trilliums, black-stemmed bamboos and the Black Knight Fritillary from Kamchatka. The spathes of the Cretan Dragon Arum peopled a grove of willows with funereal shades.

Mr Tod's house – for that was the name of the proprietor – was an airy pavilion built on a knoll about one hundred yards from the water. It was thirty-five feet square, aligned to the cardinal points, and had five sash windows on each face except for the north. The walls were of battened vertical planks painted the colour of pewter. The glazing bars were a warm ivory.

No structure could be simpler. It owed its severity and perfect proportions to the utopian projects of Ledoux and the houses of Shaker communities in New York State. The only attempt at decoration lay in two thin strips of beading round the window frames, one painted a dark lapis, the other a dry red.

Yet the architect had avoided the absolute regularity of the Western tradition. The roof was *slightly* hipped in the Chinese manner; none of the walls were *precisely* the same length; all were *fractionally* inclined inwards; and these marginal assymetries gave the building an air of movement in repose.

The doorstep was a slab of grey schist, chamfered at the corners and embedded with balas rubies. A bed of rue had been planted to conceal the foundations and the glaucous foliage seemed to lift the house above the ground.

At the foot of the knoll was a wooden pillar, ten feet high and lacquered cinnabar red. Hitched to it with a green rein was a light bay Turkoman stallion. The saddle was of the Mongolian type, of yellow leather, with base silver stirrups.

A boy came out of the house with a peregrine falcon on his gauntlet. He wore a collarless shirt of grey silk, snuff-brown breeches and red leather boots crinkled like a concertina. His grey eyes looked only into the eyes of the bird. He mounted and cantered off westwards towards a cleft in the mountain wall.

A second path led over a cloud-blue bridge that arched over the stream into a pasture. A range of buildings showed up indistinctly from behind a smokescreen of white poplars. Nearby was the black neo-classical pigeon house where Mr Tod was in the habit of training his favourite birds to imitate the dances of Sufi dervishes in trance.

On such occasions he would wear boots of canvas and rawhide elk and a *hubertusmantel* of light grey loden cloth. He was an athletic man of about fifty-five ... but it is not my intention to describe his appearance in this memoir.

All the interior walls of his house were painted an ivory-coloured tempera.

The shutters were grey: there were no curtains.

The hall was lit by a Swedish chandelier with amber instead of crystal drops. The floor was a pebble mosaic of jasper and chalcedony from the screes of the volcano. Laid out on a trestle table were two Purdey shotguns and a pair of Napoleonic green morocco dispatch boxes, one now used for cartridges, the other for trout flies. Around the walls was an arrangement *en trophée* of split cane rods, gaffs and Mr Tod's archery equipment: a yew-wood bow made for the Chevalier de Monville in 1788, a Mongolian double-reflex bow, and a Japanese samurai target of the Muromachi.

A pair of Austrian ice-axes were crossed about the lightest imaginable rucksack, stitched from strips of seal bladder and lashed to a frame of laminated birch.

The kitchen and bathroom were purely functional, the only evidence of luxury being a set of silver-lidded toilet pots made of imperial porphyry. Apart from some built-in cupboards, the rest of the house was a single room, heated by a Rostrand stove of white faience tiles. The floor was a parquet of scrubbed pine. The rug was Tibetan and blue.

At the eastern end of the room there was a screen covered with the palest orange Hawaiian tapa-cloth and, behind it, Marshal Ney's steel campaign bed with its original lime green taffeta hangings.

On the back of the screen hung the few watercolours and

drawings, salvaged from a far larger collection and which Mr Tod did not now absolutely loathe. Among them were: *The Horsehair Standards of Suleiman the Magnificent*, by the German draughtsman Melchior Lorch; *The Mechanics of an Eagle's Wing*, by Jacopo Ligozzi; a miniature of an Arctic Tern done by Mansur for the Emperor Jahangîr; a few brushstrokes of the quarry at Bibémus; an ice-floe by Caspar David Friedrich; Delacroix's own rumpled bed-sheets, and one of Turner's 'colour beginnings' – two crimson clouds in a golden sky.

Apart from a steel *chaise de camp* and Baron Vivant-Denon's travelling desk, the furniture of the room was of no consequence. Mr Tod said he had no time for furniture that would not fit on the pannier of a mule.

There were, however, two wing chairs with *decisively* cut linen covers. And on three grey tempera tables were arranged the collection of curiosities that Mr Tod, by a process of elimination and the exigencies of travel, had reduced to the bleak essentials.

In none of the works of art was the human image to be found.

Inventories make tiresome reading, so I shall confine the list to a Shang bronze fang-i with the 'melon-skin' patina; a Nuremberg sorcerer's mirror; an Aztec plate with a purple bloom; the crystal reliquary of a Gandharan stupa; a gold mounted bezoar; a jade flute; a wampum belt; a pink granite Horus falcon of Dynasty I and some Eskimo morse ivory animals which, for all the stylised attenuation of their features, seemed positively to breathe. I must, however, single out three cutting implements since they were the subject of Maximilan Tod's essay *Die Ästhetik der Messerschärfe*, published in Jena in 1941, in which he claimed that *all* weapons are artificial claws or canines and give their users the satisfaction known to carnivores as they rend warm flesh.

These were:

1 An Acheulian flint hand-axe from the Seine Gravels with the

added attraction of Louis Quinze ormolu mounts and the dedication, 'Pour le Roi'.

2 A German Bronze-Age dagger excavated by Mr Tod's father from a tumulus at Ueckermünde on the Baltic.

3 A sword blade from the collection of his friend and teacher, Ernst Gruenwald, dated 1279 and signed by Toshiru Yoshimitsu, the greatest swordsmith of Mediaeval Japan. (A mark on the blade signified that it had successfully performed, on a criminal, the movement known as *iai*, an upward thrust that severs the body clean from the right hip to the left shoulder.)

Nor shall I omit a description of three other items from the Gruenwald Collection: a tea bowl by Koetsu called 'Mountains in Winter', a box of woven birchbark from the Gold Tribe of Manchuria, and a block of blue-black stone with green markings and the inscription: '*This inkstone with Dead Eyes comes from the Old Pit of the Lower Cliff at Tuan Hsi and was the property of the painter Mi Fei.*'

In the bark box Mr Tod kept his two most treasured possessions: a calligraphy by the Zen Master, Sen Sotan, with the tenet: 'Man originally possesses nothing', and a landscape scroll by Mi Fei himself – painter of cloud-like mountains and mountain-like clouds, drunk, petromaniac, connoisseur of inkstones, hater of domesticated animals, who roamed about the mountains with his priceless art collection always beside him.

The walls of the room were bare but for a framed Turkish calligraphy, written on a gilded skeleton leaf with a line from Rûmi (Mathnâvi VI, 723): 'To be a dead man walking, one who has died before his death.'

Mr Tod's library – the visible part of it at least – was not a library in the usual sense but a collection of texts that held for him some special significance. They were bound in grey papers and kept in a shagreen travelling box. I shall itemise the order of their arrangement, since this order itself furnishes a measure of insight into their owner's character: Cassian's treatise on Accidie; the Early Irish Poem *The Hermit's Hut*; Hsien Yin Lung's Poetic *Essay on Living in the Mountains*; a facsimile of the *De Arte Venandi Cum Avibus* by the Emperor Frederick II; Abu'l Fazl's account of Akbar's pigeon flying; John Tyndall's *Notes on the Colour of Water and Ice*; Hugo von Hofmannsthal's *The Irony of Things; Landor's Cottage* by Poe; Wolfgang Hammerli's *Pilgrimage of Cain*; Baudelaire's prose poem with the English title *Any where out of the World* and the 1840 edition of Louis Agassiz's *Étude sur les Glaciers* with the appendix of chromolithographs of the Jungfrau and other Swiss glaciers.

It should be clear, even to the most unobservant reader, that I am Maximilian Tod. My history is unimportant. I detest confidences. Besides, I believe that a man is the sum of his things, even if a few fortunate men are the sum of an absence of things. Yet a few facts of my existence may help pattern my acquisitions into a chronological sequence.

I was born on 13 March 1921 in the granite mansion of my American forebears at Bucksport, Maine. (The house contained an indifferent portrait by Copley and a collection of Attic vases that did not, even as a child, excite my cupidity.) My father was Caleb Saltonstall Todd and my mother Maria Grafin Henkel von Trotschke of Ueckermünde in East Prussia. The Todds of Bucksport owed their fortune to the export of ice to India. My German ancestors stepped into history in the aftermath of the Mongol invasions. My father was a disciple of Madison Grant and was forever quoting from that author's *The Passing of the Great Race*. As an undergraduate of the Harvard Class of 1910 he read and swallowed the racial philosophy of Ernst Haeckel, whose attempts to explain history in terms of a crude biological determinism are an affront to logic and common sense.

Caleb Todd first went to Germany in 1912 where his looks won him many admirers and his charm concealed a mind of exceptional vacuity. At Harvard he had become interested in archaeology and, after reading Kossinna's inflated chronology of the German Bronze Age, seriously believed that the Aryan Race had occurred, spontaneously, on Lüneburg Heath. He stayed in America for the duration of the War, but went back to Germany in 1919. While excavating the tumulus on the Von Trotschke's estate, he met my mother and married her.

The summers of my childhood were divided between Maine and the vast neo-classical house at Ueckermünde, with its view of marsh and sky and its atrium of frigid marble goddesses. I can date my enthusiasm for blue ice to a visit to the Hamburg Kunsthalle in 1930 where I saw Friedrich's masterpiece *The Wreck of the Hope*. I confirmed this passion in 1934 when I first set eyes on the pinnacles and 'chimneys' of the Lower Grindelwald Glacier.

My mother drowned in a yachting accident in the Gulf of Bothnia in June 1938, the consequence of my father's cowardice and lack of seamanship. I never saw him again.

My education had been entrusted to private tutors: as a result I was entirely self-educated. In May 1937 I published the first of my art-historical essays, on Altdorfer's *Alexanderschlacht* in Munich. Some months before I had bought from an antiquaire in the rue du Bac the steel easel on which Napoleon had the picture wheeled into his bathroom at Malmaison. My theme was the expression in the eye of Darius, horrified yet amorous, as he sees the tip of Alexander's lance aimed at him through the furious mêlée of the battle.

I was in Innsbruck when war was declared, taking notes for an article on the Archduke Ferdinand's Wunderkammer at Schloss Ambras. I knew the United States would fight with the Allies, and hurried to Berlin. Through the influence of my grandfather I became a citizen of the Reich.

My reasons for choosing Germany were aesthetic. I believed that war is Man's supreme aesthetic experience and that only the Germans and Japanese understood this. Only they understood the texture of war: it was unthinkable to fight on the other side.

Not that I or my friends expected to win. We never shared the hysterical optimism of the High Command. We fought for reasons inexplicable to those opportunist parvenus: for us, Bolshevism and National Socialism were facets of the same phenomenon. Nor did we fight for the Fatherland. We fought only to fight. We fought, in fact, to lose. Aesthetically, it is always safer to lose.

In Berlin I made friends with Ernst Gruenwald, the Secretary of the German-Japanese Friendship Society. He had lived thirty years in Japan, ten of them in the Daitoku-ji Monastery in Kyoto. He alone in the west understood the quality in art the Japanese call 'wabi'. Literally the word means 'poverty', but applied to a work of art it means that true beauty, 'the beauty that breaks away from this world', must rely on the use of its humblest materials.

I went to live with Gruenwald at his country house near Eberswalde. That summer, intoxicated by the scent of late-flowering lindens, we practised Zen archery while, outside the gates, tanks rumbled along the road to Poland.

In December 1940 I joined the 24th Panzer Korps; in the following summer we invaded the Ukraine. I could squeeze few luxuries into my tank, but did manage to take my Purdeys, some volumes of Voltaire and my smoking jacket. My friend Rainer von Hagenburg and I had agreed to attend the first night of the renamed Bolshoi Ballet in civilian dress – a performance we knew would never take place.

No aspect of the invasion disappointed me: the excellence of wildfowl shooting in the Pripet Marshes; the oxyhydrogen flares of the flame-throwers; the yellow shield of a dead Mongol's face; the Soviet loudspeakers blaring the Budenny March over long-abandoned wheatfields; the drawn but happy faces of the aristocrats who greeted us after twenty-four years of living death.

On 12 September 1942, at our assault on Stalingrad, a bullet caught me in the groin. Laid out on a field stretcher I removed the final 'd' from my name. And yet I recovered from the operation. Von Hagenburg even recovered my Voltaire and my Purdeys. I returned, an invalid, to Berlin.

The next summer found me in Finland in my capacity as expert on the fracture of ice. At Rovaniemi I met Vaino Mustanoja, a man whose tastes corresponded so precisely with my own. His description of the Patagonian glaciers fired me with longing for the Far South. I envied his collection of Eskimo artefacts.

Mustanoja had built a Doric pavilion in the forest. Inside and out were painted black and stencilled with silver tears in memory of the room decorated by the regicide St Just at Rheims. Here, with the light of white nights flickering through the birches, we dined on gravlax, smoked reindeer fillet and cloudberries, our conversations unexhausted by the morning. Here also I witnessed his sad end.

As late as November 1944 the Führer was importing porphyry columns from Sweden, doubtless intended for some monument to himself, doubtless unaware that Swedish porphyry is not an acceptable substitute for Egyptian. His geologists were incapable of choosing stone of good quality. My services were accepted. I left for Stockholm, taking with me the finest pieces of the Gruenwald Collection, saving them from certain destruction. Through an intermediary I gave the Crown Prince a stem cup that had belonged to the Emperor Hsuan Tsang. I was granted asylum. The cup was no loss: it was, in my opinion, the only lapse in Gruenwald's taste.

In 1945 I became an Argentine citizen and under the pseudonym of Mills began my academic career as a glaciologist.

Eventually I returned to the United States, where, from minor colleges, I assembled a portfolio of pointless distinctions.

I began work on my 'refined Thebaid' in the southern summer of 1947–8, believing at the time that nuclear war was inevitable in the Northern Hemisphere. In the years that followed I spent at least three months in my valley, but by 1960 inflation, the cost of freight and the blackmailing demands of Chilean and Argentine officials had eaten into the capital I had placed in Swiss banks.

I met Estelle Neumann in the Peabody Museum in 1962 as she was admiring a case of glass flowers. She said she came from Trenton, New Jersey. I was surprised, neither by Trenton nor her admiration for the flowers. I found in her an ideal mixture of brilliance and incredible stupidity. No original thought entered her head, yet she did have the wit to appropriate each one of my suggestions as her own.

But now my schemes have not turned out as planned. I am writing this memoir in a tin shack in the Atacama Desert. My water is running low. I had intended to settle for ever in my valley; I have left it for others to pillage. I have left my young companion. I have left my things. I, who with bedouin rigour abolished the human form from my possessions … I, who did everything to protect my retina from the visual affronts of the twentieth century, now I too am prey to hallucinations. Women with red faces leer at me. Wet lips slaver over me. Monstrous blocs of colour smother me. Je dus voyager, *distraire les enchantements assemblés dans mon cerveau.* One particular colour continues to torment me: the orange of Estelle Neumann's anorak the second before I pushed her.

1979

BEDOUINS

*... and dwell in tents that ye may live long in the
land where ye are strangers.*

Jeremiah

He was travelling to see his old father who was a rabbi in Vienna.
His skin was white. He had a small fair moustache and bloodshot
eyes, the eyes of a textual scholar. He held up a grey serge
overcoat, not knowing where to hang it. He was very shy. He was
so shy that he could not undress with anyone else in the
compartment.

I went into the corridor. The train was speeding up. The lights
of Frankfurt disappeared into the night.

Five minutes later he was lying on the upper bunk, relaxed and
eager to talk. He had studied at a Talmudic Academy in Brooklyn.
His father had left America fifteen years earlier: the morning
would reunite them.

He and his father disapproved of America. They mistrusted the
Zionist mood. Israel was an idea, not a country. Besides, Jahweh
gave the Land for his Children to wander through, not to settle or
sink roots there.

Before the war his family had lived in Sibiu in Romania. When
the war came they hoped they were safe; then, in 1942, Nazis set a
mark on the house.

The father shaved his beard and cut his ringlets. His Gentile servant fetched him a peasant costume, black breaches and a smocked linen shirt. He took his first-born son and ran into the woods.

The Nazis took the mother, the sisters and the baby boy. They died in Dachau. The rabbi walked through the Carpathian beech forests with his son. Shepherds sheltered him and gave him meat. The way the shepherds slaughtered sheep did not offend his principles. Finally, he crossed the Turkish frontier and made his way to America.

Now father and son were returning to Romania. Recently they had a sign, pointing the way back. Late one night, in his apartment in Vienna, the rabbi reluctantly answered the doorbell. On the landing stood an old woman with a shopping basket.

She said, 'I have found you.'

She had blue lips and wispy hair. Dimly he recognised his Gentile servant.

'The house is safe,' she said. 'Forgive me. For years I pretended it was now a Gentile house. Your clothes are there, your books even. I am dying. Here is the key.'

'All houses are Gentile houses,' the rabbi said.

1978

III

'THE NOMADIC ALTERNATIVE'

LETTER TO TOM MASCHLER

24th February, 1969

Dear Tom,

   You asked me to write you a letter about my proposed book on nomads. I cannot provide a history of nomads. It would take years to write. In any case I want the book to be general rather than specialist in tone. The question I will try to answer is 'Why do men wander rather than sit still?' I have proposed one title – *The Nomadic Alternative*. We obviously won't use it. It is too rational a title for a subject that appeals to irrational instincts. For the moment it has the advantage of implying that the nomad's life is not inferior to the city dweller's. I have to try and see the nomads as they see themselves, looking outwards at civilisation with envy or mistrust. By civilisation I mean 'life in cities', and by civilised those who live within the ambit of literate urban civilisation. All civilisations are based on regimentation and rational behaviour. Nomads are uncivilised and all the words traditionally used in connection with them are charged with civilised prejudices – vagrant, vagabond, shifty, barbarian, savage, etc. Wandering nomads are bound to be a disruptive influence but they have been blamed out of all proportion to the material damage they cause. This blame is rationalised and justified by false piety. The nomads are excluded; they are outcasts. Cain 'wandered over the surface of the earth'.

The first chapter might ask the question – Why wander? It could start with the Greek legend of Io and her compulsive wandering, and be called 'Io's Gadfly' (if that's not too trite). The word 'nomad' comes from words meaning 'to pasture' but it has come to apply to the earliest hunters as well. Hunters and herdsmen shift for economic reasons. Less obvious are the reasons for the nomad's intransigence in face of settlement even when the economic inducements are overwhelmingly in its favour. But the mutual antagonism of citizen and nomad is only one half of the theme. The other is much nearer home – ESCAPISM (a good personal reason for writing the book). Why do I become restless after a month in a single place, unbearable after two? (I am, I admit, a bad case.) Some travel for business. But there is no economic reason for me to go, and every reason to stay put. My motives, then, are materially irrational. What is this neurotic restlessness, the gadfly that tormented the Greeks? Wandering may settle some of my natural curiosity and my urge to explore, but then I am tugged back by a longing for home. I have a compulsion to wander and a compulsion to return – a homing instinct like a migrating bird. True nomads have no fixed home as such; they *compensate* for this by following unalterable paths of migration. If these are upset it is usually by interference from the civilised or semi-civilised half-nomads. The result is chaos. Nomads develop exaggerated fixations about their tribal territory. 'Land is the basis of our nation. We shall fight!' said a nomad chief of the second century BC. He cheerfully gave away his best horse, all his treasure and his favourite wife, but fought to the death for a few miles of useless scrub. This obsession for tribal land lies behind the tragedy of the Near East. The High Seas do not invoke quite the same emotional response, and territorial waters lie close to land. Sailors' emotions are directed towards the feminised ship that carries them and their home port.

Looking at some of today's studies of animal and human behaviour, one can detect two trends ...

1 Wandering is a human characteristic genetically inherited from the vegetarian primates.
2 All human beings have the emotional, if not an actual biological, need for a *base*, cave, den, tribal territory, possessions or port. This is something we share with the carnivores.

Chapter II will deal with the omnivorous weapon–using ARCHAIC HUNTERS. They can be traced from the lower Palaeolithic to the present day. They *follow* their food supply; they return home to *base*. They *take*, gratefully, what nature offers (chapter title – 'Predators'?), but make no practical effort to propagate their food supply, except by ritually identifying themselves with animals or inanimate objects in their environment. Living for the moment, they are distinguished from us by having a radically different concept of time and its significance, though differences of this kind are matters of degree rather than kind. Their lives are not one long struggle for food, as many imagine. Much of their time is passed in gross idleness, particularly the Australian Aboriginals whose dialectic arguments know no bounds of complication. Though capable of bouts of intense concentration while actually getting their food supply, they do not take kindly to manual work. The leaders lead; they do not coerce. The whole point of receiving a gift is to give it away; a pair of trousers given to an Aboriginal will pass rapidly through twenty hands and end up decorating a tree. Vendetta is a private rather than a public affair. If they kill one another, it is usually for ritual reasons. Mass extermination is a speciality of the civilised. The

'Neo-barbarism' of Hitler was Civilisation in its most vicious aspect.

Chapter III will be a discussion of Civilisation (as something to escape from). Chapter title – 'The Comforts of Literacy'. 'Put writing in your heart. Thus you may protect yourself from any kind of labour' – Egyptian scribe to his son *c.* 2400 BC. The triumph of the white-collar worker was achieved over the backs of sweated labour. The Civilisations of the Old World crystallised in river valleys where the soil was fertile but the choice was 'Make dams or be swept out to sea'. Note the hero's medals offered *posthumously* by a grateful Mao to those 'human dams' drowned while blocking the Hwang-Ho in spate. Diffusionism is unfashionable but I believe (with Lewis among others) that Civilisation as such was an accident that happened once and once only in the very peculiar conditions of Southern Iraq, and that the consequences of this 'accident' spread as far as the Andes before Columbus. This proposition is highly debatable. On it hinges the question 'Is Civilisation something natural – a state to which many different cultures have irrevocably led?' 'Are those that did not failures – or are they alternatives to Civilisation?' 'Or is Civilisation an anti-natural accident?' If so, the evolutionary analogies, of Darwinism and the survival of the fittest, are misapplied when used with reference to human cultures. In any case *writing* develops hand in hand with specialisation, standardisation and bureaucracy, and with them a stratified social and economic hierarchy, and the repression of one group by a ruling minority. The first written tablets record how much the slaves are bringing in. Literate Civilisation freed some for the higher exercises of the mind, for the development of logical thought, mathematics, practical medicine based on scientific observation rather than faith healing etc. But in Mesopotamia the two highest gods were Anu (Order) and Enlil (Compulsion). Breasted writes of the 'dauntless

78

courage of the architect of the Great Pyramid'. However, the 2.5 million blocks were hauled up by fettered labour. Civilisation was *lashed* into place. We inherit the load.

Chapter IV 'Herdsmen' (or 'Pastoralists').

The herding of domesticated animals was one of the technical advances that led towards the formation of Civilisation, but it was always combined with some sort of agriculture, and was, therefore, always reasonably settled. True pastoral nomadism, with herds on the move all the time and no agriculture, was not a stage towards Civilisation. It developed as an *alternative* to it. It was directly in competition with it, especially in border regions. The art of riding provided the means of mobility; it was the 'tip-over' factor that enabled some groups to abandon agriculture and be permanently on the move. The pastoralist had much in common with the hunter – they believed in a mystical bond between animal and man. But from Civilisation they learned the idea of the unity of the State, and from the techniques of herding and killing domesticated animals, they discovered those of human coercion and extermination.

This is a long chapter and perhaps best divided into two. I will then trace the origins of the great nomad cultures, the Scythians, the Huns, the Germanic 'waves', the Dorian Greeks, the Arabs, the Mongols and the Turks, the last (semi)nomadic people to aspire to world conquest.

There will be an account of nomadic life; its harshness and intolerance, its illiteracy and obsession with genealogies; the comparative lack of slavery, though that did not prevent nomads from being the most successful slave traders; the renunciation of all but the most portable possessions in times of emergency; the failure to appreciate civilised standards of human life balanced by a natural adjustment towards death, which the super-civilised have lost; the communality of property and land within a tribe. 'All are

God's guests. We share and share alike' (Bedou chief); the position of women (remarkably emancipated, particularly in Northern Asia); the sanctity of the craftsman etc.

Chapter V will continue the story of the nomads in face of a triumphant agricultural and then industrial Civilisation. I may call it ' "Civilisation or Death!" ' the cry of the American frontiersman. This will be a record of the hard line towards nomads, its rationalised hatred and self-assumed moral superiority. Nomads are equated with animals, and treated as such. I will discuss the fate of the Gypsies, the American Indians, the Lapps and the Zulus, also nomads within highly civilised societies, tramps, hobos etc. I would give an account of the Beja in the Eastern Sudan, the Fuzzy-Wuzzies of Kipling. They have been able to resist all civilising influences, since they were first mentioned in Egyptian annals some three thousand years ago, only because they are prepared to tolerate the lowest level of personal comfort. They are sensationally idle and truculent as well. Most of the morning for the men is taken up by a fantastic mutual coiffure session (grooming urge?). There is also the depressing moral and physical effect of Civilisation on the Arab. 'Law and order have settled in like a blight on Sinai and Palestine' (G. W. Murray, *The Sons of Ishmael*).

Chapter VI will be the reverse of Chapter V and will trace the longings of civilised men for a natural life identified with that of the nomads or other 'primitive' peoples. To be called 'Nostalgia for Paradise', the belief that all those who have successfully resisted or remained unaffected by civilisation have a secret to happiness that the civilised have lost. It is bound up with the idea of the 'Fall of Man', with Paradise myths and Utopias, the Myth of the Noble Savage and primitivist writings from Hesiod on. Its most extreme form is Animalitarianism, the assumption that animals are endowed with superior moral qualities to human beings. 'I could turn and live with the animals ...' (Walt Whitman). Hence at a different level the popularity of such books as *Born Free*. Otherwise it may emphasise the essential unity of animal and man, an intellectual tendency far older than Aesop and still with us. We also have a lingering idea that eating animals is sinful, and it is interesting to find that some Asian hunting tribes preserve legends of a Vegetarian Paradise, a folk memory of our vegetarian primate days.

Chapter VII – 'The Compensations of Faith'

Nomads are hated – or adored. Why? It cannot be sheer chance that no great transcendental faith has ever been born of an Age of Reason. Civilisation is its own religion; religion and state are wedded; at the apex the god king of Egypt, the deified Roman emperor or the papal monarch. In its own day 'Pax Britannica' was a religion, and one nineteenth-century sceptic described as religion 'civilisation as inflicted on the "lower" races at the end of a Hotchkiss gun'. The great faiths renounce material wealth and the idea of progress in favour of spiritual values. Their ideologies hark back to the religious experiences of the early hunters and herdsmen – a complex of religious beliefs known as Shamanism. The shaman is the original religious mystic, androgynous and ecstatic. The nearest the Chinese have to a transcendental faith – Taoism – is 'little more than systematised shamanism'; Judaeo-Christianity, Zoroastrianism and the Hindu Buddhist traditions preserve their pastoral past (Feed my Sheep – The Lord is a Good Shepherd – The Flock of the Faithful – The Sacred Cow). Islam is the great nomadic religion. Even in the Middle Ages the ecstatic dualist cults of the Bogomils and Albigenses had their origins in Manichaeanism and the shamanic traditions of the western end of the steppes and they paved the way for the Reformation. The religious leaders of the Civilised give way to the shamanic type of religious hero, the self-destructive evangelist, the celibate, the wandering dervish or divine healer. Note the difference between the Shakers (ecstatics) who shook themselves out of existence and the Mormons (enthusiasts), who aspired to the Presidency. The nomad renounces; he reflects in his solitude; he abandons collective rituals, and cares little for the rational processes of learning or literacy. He is a man of faith.

The Jewish diaspora obviously violates every attempt to categorise it. I would think it worth a chapter to itself. Title – ? 'The Wandering Jew' – a daunting subject. There are two questions I would like to ask – Was Jewish 'exclusivism' kept alive by the loss of the 'Promised Land', their tribal territory? and were their energies diverted as a result towards the nomad's other great stand-by – portable gold?

Incidentally, while we are about it we can lay for all time the Great Aryan Myth; it surfaced again the other day in a new disguise – the wishful thinking of a frustrated lady archaeologist. Northern nomads – The Blond Brutes – were not the active masculine principle that fertilised an effete south. The Amazons are not my idea of femininity; they could not aspire to womanhood till they had killed their man. Neither are the Maenads nor the Bacchae. They were all nomad ladies. There must be some other explanation.

Chapter VIII will continue some more general aspects of nomadic behaviour, and may be called the 'Nomadic Sensibility'; their sense of values; the importance of music (the drum and guitar are pre-eminently nomadic instruments); the craving for brilliant colour and the reassuring brilliance of gold. Nomads wear the most elaborate jewellery; a Bedou woman will wear her whole fortune round her neck; the nomads' roads to ecstasy – Turkish Baths, saunas, Indian hemp and mushrooms. Nomadic art is intuitive and irrational rather than analytic and static. I could use some illustrations to make my points and this chapter will obviously be expanded as I go along.

Chapter IX to be called the 'Nomadic Alternative' calls into question the whole basis for Civilisation, and is concerned with the present and future as much as the past. There have been two main inducements to wander: ECONOMIC and NEUROTIC. For example, the International Set are neurotics. They have reached satiation point at home; so they wander – from tax-haven to tax-haven with an occasional raid on the source of their wealth – their *base*. How often has one heard the lamentations of an American expatriate at the prospect of a visit to his trustees in Pittsburgh. The same thing happened in the Roman Empire in the third century AD and later. The rich abdicated the responsibilities of their wealth; the cities became unendurable and at the mercy of property speculators. Wealth was divorced from its sources. A strong state took over and collapsed under the strain. The rich wore their wealth, and the governments passed endless laws against extravagance in dress. Compare the diamonds and gold boxes of today, and the aura attached to portable possessions. The mobile rich were impossible to tax: the advantages of no-fixed-address were obvious. So the unpredictable demands of the tax-collector were laid at the feet of those who could least afford to pay. Wandering passed from the neurotic to the economic stage.

True nomads watch the passing of civilisations with equanimity; so does China, that unique combination of Civilisation and Barbarism. There is a good Egyptian text to illustrate the patronising attitude of the super-civilised in his self-confident days. 'The miserable Asiatic ... he does not live in one place but his feet wander ... he conquers not, neither is he conquered. He may plunder a lonely settlement but he will never take a populous city.' Civilisations destroy themselves; nomads have never (to my certain knowledge) destroyed one, though they are never far away at the kill, and may topple a disintegrating structure. The civilised alone have control of their destiny, and I do not believe in any of the cyclical theories of decline, fall and rebirth.

Now for today. We may have enough food even, but we certainly do not have enough room. Marshall McLuhan asks us to accept that literacy, the linch-pin of Civilisation is OUT; that electronic technology is by-passing the 'rational processes of learning' and that jobs and *specialists* are things of the past. 'The World has become a Global Village,' he says. Or is it Mobile Encampment? 'The expert is the man who *stays put.*' Literature, he says will disappear, and the social barriers are coming down; everyone is free for the higher exercises of the mind (or spirit?). One thing is certain – the Paterfamilias, that bastion of Civilisation (not the matriarch) is right OUT. McLuhan is correct in much of his analysis of the effects of the new media. He does not seem to appreciate their probable long-term consequences. They are likely to be rather less than comfortable. The old nostalgic dream of a free classless society may indeed now be possible. But there are too many of us and there would have to be a drastic drop in population. Much of the world's population is on the move as never before, tourists, businessmen, itinerant labour, drop-outs, political activists, etc: like the nomads who first sat on a horse, we have again the means for total mobility. As anyone who owns a house knows, it is often cheaper to move than to stay. But this new Internationalism has activated a new parochialism. Separatism is rampant. Minorities feel threatened; small exclusive groups splinter off. The £50 travel allowance was not imposed for purely economic reasons.

Are these two trends not representative of the two basic human characteristics I mentioned earlier?

Yours ever,

Bruce Chatwin

THE NOMADIC
ALTERNATIVE

Diogenes the Cynic said that men first crowded into cities to escape the fury of those outside. Locked within their walls, they committed every outrage against one another as if this were the sole object of their coming together. Diogenes' deprecation of city life is an early example of 'cultural primitivism' or 'the discontent of the civilised with civilisation'.[1] It is an emotional rather than a rational impulse that has always led men to abandon civilisation and seek a simpler life, a life in harmony with 'nature', unhampered with possessions, free from the grinding bonds of technology, sinless, promiscuous, anarchic, and sometimes vegetarian.

But civilisation rarely lacks its champions. 'All men have civic virtues,' as Protagoras suggested – 'a democratic note often in modern times associated with the belief that democracy is a return to the original goodness of man.'[2] The word 'civilisation' is charged with moral and ethical overtones, the accumulated inheritance of our own self-esteem. We contrast it with barbarism, savagery, and even bestiality, whereas it means nothing more than 'living in cities'. The City, as such, appeared with astonishing

---

[1] Arthur O. Lovejoy and George Boas, *Primitivism and Related Ideas in Antiquity* (repr. Octagon Books, 1965), p. 7.
[2] Ibid., p. 210.

abruptness out of the alluvium of Southern Mesopotamia in the late fourth millennium BC. This transformation depended on irrigation works, intensive agriculture, specialised skills such as pottery and metallurgy, and supervision by a literate bureaucracy, judiciary and priesthood. Civilisation demands a stratified social and economic hierarchy. There is, regrettably, no indication that it is cohesive without one. The urban civilisations of the Old World radiated outwards, excluding all who would not conform to the canons of civilised behaviour. There were setbacks. Mesopotamian chroniclers lament the ravages of the 'Amorite who knows not the grain' or the 'host whose onslaught is like a hurricane, a people who have never known a city'.[1] But as the civilisations consolidated they came, in the north, to the point of diminishing returns. Their natural frontiers crystallised. Beyond, the 'barbarians' were to be left to their own devices. As some Han officials said, 'The lands are all swamps and saline waters, not fit for habitation. It is better to make peace.'[2] But the stigmatised outsider was unlikely to regard the frontier with the smugness of the man inside; nor could he emulate urban civilisation in land unsuited to it. On the steppe, from Mongolia to Hungary and beyond, he gave up his agriculture and opted for a 'Nomadic Alternative'.[3]

A nomad does not 'wander aimlessly from place to place' as one dictionary would have it. The word derives from the Latin and Greek meaning 'to pasture'. Pastoral tribes follow the most conservative patterns of migration, changing them only in times of drought or disaster. The animals provide their food; agriculture, trade or plunder are additional benefits. 'The Nomad' is a clan

---

[1] C. J. Gadd, 'The Dynasty of Agade and the Gutian Invasion', *The Cambridge Ancient History*, rev. edn, (Cambridge, 1963), vol. I, ch. XIX.

[2] Ssu-Ma-Ch'ien, *Records of the Grand Historian of China (Shih Chi)*, trans. B. Watson (New York and London, 1961), ch. 110, p. 169.

[3] For pastoral nomadism see O. Lattimore, *Inner Asian Frontiers of China*, reprint (New York, 1962), p. 238 ff.

elder, responsible to the whole tribe, who parcels out the grazing for each person. Ssu-Ma-Ch'ien says that the Hsiung-nu congregated in the first month of the year for the allotment of their rights, and again in the autumn when the cattle were fat. Haymaking does not enter into this scheme: that would prejudice mobility and grazing claims. Spring and summer are the times when the nomads are on the move. 'The days are long and the nights are short,' a Chinese said of the plains about the Caspian in the thirteenth century: 'in little more than the time needed to cook a mutton chop, the sun rises again.'[1]

The nomads selected their animals to make the best use of all types of pasture. Horses and cattle cannot graze where sheep and goats have already cropped; herdsmen must move to keep their animals from starving. Heavy oxcarts are known from the steppe from the third millennium BC, the progenitors of the Scythian wagons, 'the smallest with four wheels, the largest with six, all covered over with felt'.[2] But equitation, adopted some thousand years later, so increased the nomads' range that they could abandon their unprofitable agriculture completely. All known species of horse can hybridise with one another; there are two distinct species involved in domestication: the one the steppe ponies of Tarpan and Przevalski's type, the other the 'cold-blooded' European forest horse. When riding horses first appear in graves near the Danube they resemble Przevalski's horse, a species confined in the wild to Mongolia. Central Asia bred the finest horses, the 'Celestial Horses' of Ferghana that fed on fields of blue alfalfa, or the 'hoar-frost' coloured chargers of the Alans. The Emperor Hadrian had an Alanic horse that 'flew' and he named it Caesar. The steppe came to resemble a vast exercise ground with squadrons of cavalry moving up and down it.

---

[1] E. Bretschneider, *Mediaeval Researches from Eastern Asiatic Sources* (London, 1910), vol. I, p. 25.
[2] Hippocrates, *Airs, Waters and Places*, xvii.

The nomad had a tactical advantage over the farmer. He could descend and pasture his horses on the irrigated fields. After the Great Wall of China was built, the Hsiung-nu 'no longer ventured to come south to pasture their horses'. But if the defences were unmanned, they demanded tribute or threatened: 'When autumn comes we will take our horses and trample your crops.'[1] The same problem faced the Romans on the Rhine and Danube limes. Nomad and citizen belonged to exclusive systems and both knew it.

But a pastoralist is a poor man. He could not always resist the temptations of trade or plunder that brought the luxuries of civilisation. The steppe is brilliant with spring flowers in May. At other seasons the featureless landscape is dry and dusty or leaden with frost and snow. The nomad craves colour. He is also traditionally drawn to the reassuring brilliance of gold. 'The Huns burned with an insatiable lust for gold,' wrote Ammianus Marcellinus.[2] He spoke of their 'hideous clothes', and Apollinaris Sidonius was overcome by the garish outfits of the young Frankish prince Sigismer, 'a flame red mantle with much glint of ruddy gold … feet laced in bristly hide … and green cloaks with crimson borders'.[3]

Luxury hampers mobility. The nomad leaders knew that over-indulgence threatened their system. Civilised ways were insidious. Attila drank from a wooden cup and Chingis Khan lived in a yurt to the end of his days. Like so many colonists, the Greeks brought drink to the lands they colonised. Herodotus tells the sad tale of the Scythian king, Scyles. Discovering the delights of Bacchus, he was 'maddened' by the god. The Scythians, however, were intolerant of such innovations and demanded conformity. They beheaded their king. They also shot Anacharsis, a Scythian

---

[1] Ssu-Ma-Ch'ien, op. cit., ch. 48.
[2] Marcellinus, *History*, xxxi, 2. 10.
[3] Sidonius, *Letter* xx.

divine healer or shaman, who wandered through Greece 'carrying a small drum and hanging himself about with images'.[1] At Cyzicus he worshipped the Great Goddess, and the Greeks admired him for his spirituality. 'And now,' says Herodotus, 'the Scythians say they have no knowledge about him; this is because he left his country and followed the customs of strangers.'

There were, however, obvious attractions for the city dweller in a society where 'all are born noble' and where there was less slavery (for it was too troublesome). In times of despair the 'Nomadic Alternative' was too tempting to resist. A Han counsellor, Yin Shan, was appalled at the prospect of a proposed abandonment of the Great Wall. 'The frontier posts of China are as much needed to keep the Chinese traitors out of the Tartar's land as keeping the Tartars out of China.'[2] The eunuch Chung-hsing-sho, a defector to the Hsiung-nu, decried the complications of city life, its useless silks, elaborate food, ornate houses and tiresome social obligations; he contrasted them with the simplicity of felt and leather clothing, comradeship, cheese and plain meat. Similarly a Greek, once married to a rich woman, ran away to the Huns. With tears in his eyes he admitted that the Roman constitution was the best in the world but claimed that the complacency of its rulers, the tyranny of its generals, the inequity of its legal expenses and the unpredictable burdens of its taxation had ruined it. Nomads rarely, if ever, destroyed a civilisation. They merely took advantage of a disintegrating situation. In this they were encouraged by defectors or uncommitted nomads, who were the disruptive factor in steppe politics.

The military tactics of the steppe horsemen and those of civilised states were incompatible. Once the steppe ponies passed into agricultural lands their short legs bogged down. Conversely it

[1] Herodotus iv, 76–80.
[2] E. H. Parker, *One Thousand Years of the Tartars*, 2nd cdn rev. (New York, 1924), p. 49.

was only in times of national prosperity and outstanding leadership that any great power could countenance the hideous expense of a mounted expedition against the 'natural cavalry' of the steppe. 'No profit comes to an army that has to fight a thousand miles from home,' the Imperial Secretary lamented.[1] What was worse, the nomads ran away. The Celts taunted their foes and rushed into battle. The Scythians or the Huns did nothing so inept. 'They do not consider it a disgrace to run away. Their only concern is self-advantage, and they know nothing of propriety or righteousness,'[2] the assumption, so recurrent in our time, that the enemy is obliged to show its face.

Part of Herodotus' Book iv reads like a manual for guerilla warfare. 'They [the Scythians] have devised that none who attack them can escape, and none catch them if they desire not to be found. For when men have no stabilised cities or fortresses, but are all house-bearers and mounted archers, living not by tilling the soil but by raising cattle and carrying their dwellings on wagons, how should they not be invincible and unapproachable.'[3] Darius invaded Scythia in 516 BC with a conventional army. He chased around Russia, probably as far north as Kazan on the Volga, the Scythians always retreating before him. In exasperation he sent a message to their king. 'Why do you always run away? Why don't you stand and fight or else submit?' The reply, 'I have never fled for fear of any man, nor do I now flee from you. If you really want a fight, find the graves of our fathers, and then you'll see whether we'll fight. As for your boast that you are my master, go and cry.'[4] The retreat of Darius resembled the retreat of Napoleon; he only just escaped. Compare the tactics of Mao Tse-Tung.

The steppe nomads moved in summer. The northern tribes of

[1] Ssu-Ma-Ch'ien, op. cit, ch. 108.
[2] Ibid., ch. 110.
[3] Herodotus, iv, 46.
[4] Ibid., 126, 127.

the taiga and tundra stayed put. Swamps and swollen rivers impeded all movement, except, perhaps, when escape from the clouds of mosquitoes that make the short Arctic summer so uncomfortable was imperative. They awaited the great migrations of wild-fowl, swans, ducks and geese, clubbing them to death in moult. In some rivers the teeming runs of salmon and sturgeon provided food close to their settlements. The winter was the season for mobility, when the rivers and bogs froze, and since the Arctic Stone Age these peoples had known the use of dog- and deer-drawn sledges and skis; Ptolemy refers to the Skrithifinnoi or Skiing Finns. It was also the trapping season, for sables, marten, mink, lemming, ermine and Arctic fox. Fur was, and still is, the staple of the Siberian tribes. The heroes of the Nibelungenlied wallowed in their sables; Kubilai Khan had a tent lined with ermine and sable, and the Cossack colonists of Boris Goudonov greeted the Kirghiz with cries of 'Sables or Death!'

Following their passion for human urine, reindeer were attracted to human settlement. They were easily tamed, could be ridden and harnessed. They provided meat, milk and hides. The elk was also ridden, and it was once claimed that reindeer- and elk-riding preceded equitation. The poet of the Finnish epic, the *Kalevala*, was quite unable to decide if the hero Väinämöinen fell from his 'blue elk' or his 'dun-coloured courser';[1] this seems to be reflected in the Pazyryk burials where horses of the finest central Asiatic breed were fitted with reindeer masks. The Mongols themselves were one of the forest tribes who broke out onto the horse-riding steppe.

The condition of north Asian hunters remained virtually unchanged from prehistoric times until the nineteenth century. Their tangible remains, when recovered, testify to this tenacious conservatism. Metal-working came late to the north, and though

[1] *Kalevala*, trans. W. F. Kirby (London, 1925), rune vi, 25.

wood, leather and bone preserve well in bog conditions, their survival is less favoured than is that of the debris of civilised communities. Consequently, assessments of the Animal Style art of northern Europe and Asia may lay undue stress on influences emanating from the south. Influences there certainly were; many individual motifs can be traced back to their southern sources. But, from the Upper Palaeolithic era, the North had its own Animal Style, conserving its own peculiar conventions. These Arctic Stone Age finds include the wooden bird and animal figures from the Gorbunovo bog in the Urals, slate maces from Sweden and Finland, the bone carvings from the graves on the middle Yenisei River in Siberia, the rock carvings of animals stretching from central Siberia to Norway. Three wooden ladles from southern Finland were carved from a pine (*pinus cembra*) that grew in the Urals a thousand miles away. Those sledges certainly travelled.

To the Greeks, northern and central Asia was a Land of Darkness, a land of abominable monstrosities. Their main source of information came from an epic poem, now lost, the *Arismaspeia* by Aristeas of Proconnessus.[1] This traveller seems to have made a journey into Scythia and far beyond during the seventh century BC, in advance of the first Greek settlements on the northern coast of the Black Sea. Some say his was a journey of the spirit, a 'soul-journey' like a shaman's, but his topography is too circumstantial. He knew of the promiscuous Agathyrsi 'greatly given to wearing gold', the Cave of the Winds – probably the Dzungarian Gap in Western Mongolia – and the Rhipean Mountains, identified as the Altai – the 'Mountain of Rhipe, aflower with forests, breast of the black night,' wrote the Spartan poet Alcman. Thereabouts beaked griffins guarded sacred gold from the one-eyed Arismas-

[1] J. D. P. Bolton, *Aristeas of Proconnessus* (Oxford, 1962).

peians, 'the horsemen who live about Pluto's stream that flows with gold'.

Nearby, Aeschylus placed the home of the Phorcides, 'aged swan-shaped maidens possessing one eye in common and one tooth', and the three winged Gorgons 'with their snaky hair'. Long before, Hesiod knew of the Dog-Men and Herodotus of the Neuri, 'one of whom is turned into a wolf for a few days each year'. Simias in the third century BC tells of 'islands dark green with firs, overgrown with lofty reeds ... and a monstrous race of men, half dogs upon whose supple necks is set a canine head armed with powerful jaws. They bark like dogs but comprehend the speech of men.' There was a Land of Feathers; there were headless people with faces on their shoulders, the Ox-Feet, the Goat-Feet, the Web-Feet, the Parasol-Feet, and, in the Himalayas, 'hairy men swift of foot with their feet turned backwards'.[1] The Abominable Snowman is the one monstrosity that has resolutely refused to die.

The monstrosities of Asia are difficult to explain away. Some dismiss them as mythical nonsense in the same class as the 'Pobble-with-no-toes'. Others resolve them in purely ethnographical terms. The Web-Feet are wearing snow-shoes, the headless humpty-dumpties anoraks, and so on. But they are persistent. Sober Chinese annalists and the first European travellers to Central Asia in the thirteenth century report them too. The Dog Jung were nomads with whom the Chinese actually fought. 'The appearance of these people is like dogs.' There were the Kuei. 'These people have the faces of men but only one eye'; and there 'were wild men with hairy bodies and pendulous breasts'.[2] 'These are the Things from the North-East Corner to the North-West Corner,' wrote the author of the *Shan-Hai-Ching*, no later than

[1] Pliny, *Nat. Hist.*, vii, 2.
[2] Bolton, op. cit., notes to ch. iv, 7 (quotes Shan-Hai-Ching, Ssu Pu Ts-ung K'an edition, B-55/56a).

the end of the first century BC, 'the Shankless, ... the Long-Legs, ... the One-Eyes – these people have only one eye set in the middle of their forehead', and 'the Jou-Li – these people have one hand and one foot'.[1] Other sources report the 'Tip-Toes' and the 'No-Bellies'. The Annals of the Bamboo Books speak of King Mu (of the Chou Dynasty) pushing westwards over the Moving Sands (the Gobi) and the 'Country of the Heaps of Feathers'.[2] Some two thousand years later Bishop Ivo of Narbonne wrote in a panic-stricken letter that, on his invasion of Hungary, the Mongol Batu was accompanied by Dog-Headed Warriors.[3]

Civilised men attributed animal properties to the nomads. Ammianus Marcellinus spoke of the bestial cunning of the Huns – 'one might take them for two-legged beasts, or for stumps rough hewn into images'.[4] In his *Gothic History*, Jordanes wrote, 'They had a sort of lump, not a head, with pin-holes rather than eyes ... though they live in the form of men they have the cruelty of wild beasts.'[5] The Han Imperial Secretary said of the Hsiung-nu 'in their breasts beat the heart of beasts ... from the most ancient times they have never been regarded as a part of humanity'.[6] In the year I BC their ruler paid a state visit to the Chinese capital. His hosts lodged him in the Zoological Gardens.[7] In Central Asian folklore supernatural beings put their bird and animal forms on and off at will. The Lady Ala Mangnyk 'puts on her golden swan clothing'; Jelbagan's wife was a 'leaden-eyed, copper-nosed witch'; there

[1] Ibid., p. B-43a/4b.

[2] Ibid., p. 101 (quotes J. Legge, *The Chinese Classics*, vol. III, 1, p. 151).

[3] Matthew Paris, *Chronicle*, ed. H. R. Luard, Rolls Series (London, 1872–1883), vol. IV, p. 27.

[4] Ammianus Marcellinus, *History*, xxxi, 21.

[5] Jordanes, *Gothic History*, ed. C. C. Mierow (Princeton, 1915), section 127.

[6] Ssu-Ma-Ch'ien, op. cit., ch. 108.

[7] Mental attitudes die hard. A Russian Imperial Commission to the Reindeer Tungus on the Amur River wrote that 'they resemble dogs or horses, but have nothing in common with the race of men'. See Lindgren, 'North West Manchuria and the Reindeer Tungus', *Geographical Journal* 75 (1930), p. 532.

were 'swan maidens living in the dark with leaden eyes, hempen plaits, hands with yellow nails and murderous',[1] and royal emissaries in the form of hounds or eagles. Some shaman costumes are hung with ribbons that represent snakes; in the Yakut and other traditions, snakes have the same magico-religious significance as hair does. Herodotus reports a plague of snakes that drove the Neuri, the wolf tribe, from their lands; 'maybe they were sorcerers', he says.[2] Other costumes are hung with mirrors that represent little 'eyes' and little images of human organs. Tales of such curiosities may have given birth to the monsters that puzzled the Greeks; the Gorgons with their snaky hair, the swan-shaped Phorcides, griffins and Dog-Men.

Shamanism is a religious ideology peculiar to hunters and herdsmen.[3] It appears to be north Asian in origin, yet is diffused throughout North and South America, Oceania, Indonesia and Australia. Shamanist practices are historically documented in lands as far apart as China, Ireland of the Iron Age, Pagan Scandinavia, among the Scythians and Thracians, in Classical Greece after the opening of the Black Sea trade route, and even in Siberia in the nineteenth century. Its basic features are a Celestial Being identified with the Sky, direct communication between Heaven and Earth, and an infernal Region connected to these loci by a Cosmic Axis.

A shaman, as Professor E. R. Dodds describes one, is 'a psychically unstable person who has received a call to the religious life. As a result of his call he undergoes a period of rigorous training, which commonly involves solitude and fasting, and may involve a psychological change of sex. From this religious

[1] N. K. Chadwick, 'The Spiritual Ideas and Experiences of the Tartars of Central Asia', *Journal of the Royal Anthropological Institute* 66 (1936), p. 293 ff.
[2] Herodotus, iv, 105.
[3] M. Eliade, *Shamanism – Archaic Techniques of Ecstasy* (New York, 1962).

"retreat" he emerges with the power, real or assumed, of passing at will into a state of mental dissociation.'[1] Each trance repeats his symbolic death; he achieves it by fasting, followed by dancing to the monotonous beat of a drum. He often resorts to pharmaco-poeia, hemp, and the shamanic mushroom – the Fly Agaric, which is probably the Soma of Vedic texts. Ostyak and Vogul shamans eat this mushroom and fly to the Sky 'where they live in the Sun's rays like insects in human hair'.[2] Herodotus describes some Scythians 'howling for joy' in what seems to have been some kind of sauna bath with the added benefits of hemp.[3] Strabo talks of shamans or seers 'walking in smoke', and the first part of Aristophanes' Clouds seems to be little more than a moralistic take-off of a shamanistic séance.

The shaman's body 'dies', and his soul flies off on the wings of ecstasy to the Sky or to the Underworld. Dodds says, 'From these experiences, narrated by him in extempore song, he derives the skill in divination, religious poetry, and magical medicine which makes him socially important. He becomes the repository of a supernormal wisdom.'[4] Feared, sexually ambivalent, set aside from the 'normal' life of the tribe, he remains the hub of its creative activity, its culture hero.

A fable of Aesop tells of the Golden Age when 'the other animals had articulate speech, and knew the use of words; and they held meetings in the forests; and the stones spoke and needles of the pine tree ...'[5] In his trance, the shaman forsakes his human condition and regains this Paradisal Time. He identifies himself with a 'helping spirit', usually an animal or bird, and learns to

[1] E. R. Dodds, *The Greeks and The Irrational*, sixth printing (Berkeley and Los Angeles, 1968), p. 140.
[2] G. Roheim, *Hungarian and Vogul Mythology*, Monographs of the American Ethnological Society, vol. XXIII (New York, 1954), p. 51.
[3] Herodotus, iv, 74, 75.
[4] E. R. Dodds, op. cit., p. 140.
[5] Babrius, *Fab. Aesop*, Preamb. 1–13.

imitate its language. A costume completes the transformation. The Tungus have duck and reindeer costumes, the duck for ascents to the Sky, the reindeer for descents to the Underworld. By putting on the costume he becomes that animal or bird. 'I transformed myself into my holy shape of a black-throated loon and flew from tree to tree where my festival was celebrated.'[1] In the Ynglinga Saga, Odin's body 'lay as though dead, and then he became a bird, or a beast, a fish or a dragon, and went off in an instant into far-off lands'.[2] Is this the underlying idea behind the symplegma of animals, so recurrent a feature of the Animal Style?

The shaman changes himself into his alter-ego. Yet he is the focal point of all tribal activities, his protective spirit is the one which the tribe will adopt as its totem. The Teleut believe that the eagle is their protector; their words for eagle and shaman are the same. Attila was surrounded by sorcerers, and eagles were emblazoned on his shields. The undivided Turks had golden wolf-head standards. Ssu-Ma-Chi'en records that 'King Mu attacked the Ch'uan barbarians and brought back with him four white wolves and four white deer.'[3] Chingis Khan's ancestor was a wolf sent down from the sky, whose wife was a white deer. The Hungarian chronicles tell of the origin of their race: two hunters crossed the Maeotic swamp chasing a doe (the totem of those lands which they then annexed); the doe turned itself into a beautiful woman, and the sexual implications are obvious. The animal totem represents the ideal of the tribe; hence the urge to denigrate or subdue the totems of other tribes; hence one possible explanation for the 'animal combats' of the Animal Style.

Mental disorders are common in northern Asia. The harshness of the climate is sometimes blamed. Shamanist candidates, 'morbid and sensitive', tell of the relief that shamanising brings.

[1] Rohcim, op. cit., p. 51.
[2] *Ynglinga Saga*, trans. E. Monson and A.H. Smith (Cambridge, 1932), vol. VII, p. 5.
[3] Ssu-Ma-Ch'ien, op. cit., ch. 110.

The deliberate *dérèglement de tous les sens* of the shaman's ordeal stabilises an otherwise disintegrating mental condition. Periods of sanity are offset by bouts of psychosis or excursions into the world of dreams. Modern reports of hallucinations under trance include a disordering of space and form, the disintegration of eidetic images into spirals, whorls, volutes, carpet patterns, nets and lattices; colours are of otherworldly brilliance; there are half-faces, faces split in half about a central axis, X-ray vision, and 'amputated limbs, mutilated bodies, detached heads and fusion of parts'.[1]

All works of art, even mechanical artifacts, reflect the aspirations of their makers, and are eye-witnesses of the past. The art of urban civilisations tends to be static, solid and symmetrical. It is disciplined by the representation of the human body and by the mathematical skills attendant upon monumental architecture. To a greater or lesser extent, nomadic art tends to be portable, asymmetric, discordant, restless, incorporeal and intuitive. Naturalistic representations of animals, themselves often in violent motion, are combined with a compulsive tendency towards ornamentation. The northerners rarely concerned themselves with human activities, admitting only an occasional mask. Colour is violent; mass and volume are rejected in favour of bold silhouettes and a pierced technique of openwork spirals, lattices and geometric tracery. Animals are depicted from both sides at once, their heads abutted to form a frontal mask. The so-called X-ray style is common and shows a schematised view of the animal's skeleton. So is the convention of *pars pro toto*, especially with the amputated limbs of animals, and the fusion of parts to form a repertory of fantastic beasts. The similarities between hallucinatory experience and nomadic art cannot be explained away as pure chance.

In Siberia and elsewhere there was a close relationship between

[1] F. Reitman, *Psychotic Art* (London, 1950), p. 62.

the shaman, as creative personality, and the craftsman, especially the metal-smith. 'Smiths and shamans come from the same nest,' says a Yakut proverb. In nomadic society the smith was not the underprivileged artisan of civilisation; for the Mongols he was a hero and a free knight. Shamanism has always been connected with mastery over fire; metallurgical secrets are handed down within a closed circle associated with magic and sorcery. There were the Irish 'Men of Art', the Hephaestus tradition in Greece, the shaman-smiths of the *Kalevala*, and German and Japanese metallurgical secret societies.[1]

The shaman's disordered appreciation of reality verified the 'spiritual' truth of the artistic traditions of his tribe. In time, models strayed from their archetypes and became slack and repetitive. But as the shamans were able to renew the spiritual content of their beliefs, so the Animal Style was able to renew its vitality and power through to the Middle Ages and beyond.

1970

[1] M. Eliade, *The Forge and the Crucible* (New York, 1962), p. 81 ff.

IT'S A NOMAD *NOMAD* WORLD

In one of his gloomier moments Pascal said that all man's unhappiness stemmed from a single cause, his inability to remain quietly in a room. 'Notre nature,' he wrote, 'est dans le mouvement ... La seule chose qui nous console de nos misères est le divertissement.' Diversion. Distraction. Fantasy. Change of fashion, food, love and landscape. We need them as the air we breathe. Without change our brains and bodies rot. The man who sits quietly in a shuttered room is likely to be mad, tortured by hallucinations and introspection.

Some American brain specialists took encephalograph readings of travellers. They found that changes of scenery and awareness of the passage of seasons through the year stimulated the rhythms of the brain, contributing to a sense of well-being and an active purpose in life. Monotonous surroundings and tedious regular activities wove patterns which produced fatigue, nervous disorders, apathy, self-disgust and violent reactions. Hardly surprising, then, that a generation cushioned from the cold by central heating, from the heat by air-conditioning, carted in aseptic transports from one identical house or hotel to another, should feel the need for journeys of mind or body, for pep pills or tranquillisers, or for the cathartic journeys of sex, music and dance. We spend far too much time in shuttered rooms.

I prefer the cosmopolitan scepticism of Montaigne. He saw

travel as a 'profitable exercise; the mind is constantly stimulated by observing new and unknown things … No propositions astonish me, no belief offends me, however much opposed to my own … The savages who roast and eat the bodies of their dead do not scandalise me so much as those who persecute the living.' Custom, he said, and set attitudes of mind, dulled the senses and hid the true nature of things. Man is naturally curious.

'*He who does not travel does not know the value of men,*' said Ib'n Battuta, the indefatigable Arab wanderer who strolled from Tangier to China and back for the sake of it. But travel does not merely broaden the mind. It makes the mind. Our early explorations are the raw materials of our intelligence, and, on the day I write this, I see that the NSPCC suggests that children penned up in 'high-rise' flats are in danger of retarded mental development. Why did nobody think of it before?

Children need paths to explore, to take bearings on the earth in which they live, as a navigator takes bearings on familiar landmarks. If we excavate the memories of childhood, we remember the paths first, things and people second – paths down the garden, the way to school, the way round the house, corridors through the bracken or long grass. Tracking the paths of animals was the first and most important element in the education of early man.

The raw materials of Proust's imagination were the two walks round the town of Illiers where he spent his family holidays. These walks later became Méséglise and Guermantes Ways in *À la Recherche du Temps Perdu*. The hawthorn path that led to his uncle's garden became a symbol of his lost innocence. 'It was on this way', he wrote, 'that I first noticed the round shadow which apple trees cast on the sunlit ground', and later in life, drugged with caffeine and veronal, he dragged himself from his shuttered room on a rare excursion in a taxi, to see the apple trees in flower, the windows firmly shut for their smell would overpower his emotions. Evolution intended us to be travellers. Settlement for any length of time, in cave or castle, has at best been a sporadic condition in the history of man. Prolonged settlement has a vertical axis of some ten thousand years, a drop in the ocean of evolutionary time. We are travellers from birth. Our mad obsession with technological progress is a response to barriers in the way of our geographical progress.

The few 'primitive' peoples in the forgotten corners of the earth understand this simple fact about our nature better than we do. They are perpetually mobile. The golden-brown babies of the Kalahari Bushmen hunters never cry and are among the most contented babies in the world. They also grow up to be the gentlest people. They are happy with their lot, which they consider ideal, and anyone who talks of 'a murderous hunting instinct innate in man' displays his wanton ignorance.

Why do they grow up so straight? Because they are never frustrated by tortured childhoods. The mothers never sit still for long, and their babies are never left alone until the age of three and more. They lie close to their mothers' breasts in a leather sling, and are rocked into contentment by the gentle swaying walk. When a mother rocks her baby, she is imitating, unaware, the gentle savage as she walks through the grassy savannah, protecting her child from snakes, scorpions and the terrors of the bush. If we need movement from birth, how should we settle down later?

Travel must he adventurous. *'The great affair is to move,'* wrote Robert Louis Stevenson in *Travels with a Donkey*, 'to feel the needs and hitches of life more nearly; to come down off this feather bed of civilisation, and find the globe granite underfoot, and strewn with cutting flints.' The bumps are vital. They keep the adrenalin pumping round.

We all have adrenalin. We cannot drain it from our systems or pray it will evaporate. Deprived of danger we invent artificial enemies, psychosomatic illnesses, tax-collectors, and, worst of all, ourselves, if we are left alone in the single room. Adrenalin is our travel allowance. We might just as well use it up in a harmless way. Air travel is livening up in this respect but as a species we are terrestrial. Man walked and swam long before he rode or flew. Our human possibilities are best fulfilled on land or sea. Poor Icarus crashed.

The best thing is to walk. We should follow the Chinese poet Li Po in 'the hardships of travel and the many branchings of the way'. For life is a journey through a wilderness. This concept, universal to the point of banality, could not have survived unless it were biologically true. None of our revolutionary heroes is worth a thing until he has been on a good walk. Ché Guevara spoke of the 'nomadic phase' of the Cuban Revolution. Look what the Long March did for Mao Tse-Tung, or Exodus for Moses.

Movement is the best cure for melancholy, as Robert Burton (the author of *The Anatomy of Melancholy*) understood. 'The heavens themselves run continually round, the sun riseth and sets, stars and planets keep their constant motions, the air is still tossed by the winds, the waters ebb and flow ... to teach us that we should ever be in motion.' All birds and animals have biological time clocks regulated by the passage of celestial bodies. They are used as chronometers and navigation aids. Geese migrate by the stars, and some behavioural scientists have at last woken up to the fact that man is a seasonal animal. A tramp I once met best described this involuntary compulsion to wander. 'It's as though the tides was pulling you along the high road. I'm like the Arctic Tern. That's a beautiful white bird, you know, what flies from the North Pole to the South Pole and back again.'

The word 'revolution', so offensive to the persecutors of Galileo, was originally used to denote the cyclical passage of celestial bodies. When the geographical movements of people are tampered with, they attach themselves to political movements.

When a revolutionary hijacker says, 'I'm married to the Revolution,' he means it. For Revolution is a liberating god, the Dionysus of our age. It is a cure for melancholy. Revolution is the Way to Freedom, even if the end result is greater servitude.

Each spring the nomadic tribes of Asia shrug off the inertia of winter, and return with the regularity of swallows returning to their summer pastures. The women put on fresh flowered calico dresses, and literally 'wear the spring'. They sway to the rhythm of their pitching saddles, and mark time to the insistent beat of the camel bell. They look neither right nor left. Their eyes are glued to the way ahead – over the horizon. The spring migration is a ritual. It fulfils all their spiritual requirements, and the nomads are notoriously irreligious. The way up to the mountains is the path of their salvation.

The great religious teachers, Buddha in the Punjab, Christ, and Mohammed in the Near East, came among peoples whose patterns of migration had been disrupted by settlement. Islam germinated not among the tribesmen of the desert, but in the caravan cities, in the world of high finance. But 'Nobody', Mohammed said, 'becomes a prophet who was not first a shepherd.' The Hadj, Apostolic Life and the Pilgrimage to a religious centre were institutions to compensate for lack of migrations, and led to the extreme imitators of John the Baptist, 'wandering about in the desert with the wild beasts as if they themselves were animals'.

Ever since, settled people have returned to Arcadian idylls, or have sought adventure in the 'interests' of their country, misguidedly imposing on others the settlement they could not endure at home. Wanderers line the roads from here to Katmandu, but those who complain should remember the incurable student restlessness of Mediaeval Europe. The University of Paris was lucky to get through an academic year without closing. 'The students were carrying weapons,' complained one provost. 'When I came back home in the summer, from school,' said a student, 'my father hardly knew me. I was so blackened from tramping in the sun.'

All roads led to Rome, and St Bernard complained that there was not a single town in France or Italy without its quota of English whores, the pioneers of a great tradition. The Church finally became exasperated by its novices going about naked in public, sleeping in baking ovens and singing Goliardic verses with titles like 'The Oracle of the Holy Bottle'. A new order went out: 'SIT IN THY CELL and walk round the cloister only when asked to do so.' It was no use.

The Sufis spoke of themselves as 'travellers on the way' and used the same expression as the nomads used for their migration route. They also wore the nomads' woollen clothing. The ideal of a Sufi was to walk as a beggar or dance himself into a state of permanent ecstasy, 'to become a dead man walking', 'one who has died before his time'. 'The dervish', says one text, 'is a place over which something is passing, not a wayfarer following his own free will.' This sentiment is close to Walt Whitman's '*O Public Road, you express me better than I express myself* ...' The dances of the whirling dervishes imitated the movements of the sun, moon, planets and stars. 'He who knows the Dance knows God,' says Rumi.

Dervishes in ecstasy believed that they flew. Their dancing costumes were adorned with symbolic wings. Sometimes their clothes were deliberately shredded and patched. This denoted that the wearer had ripped them to bits in the fury of the dance. A fashion for patchwork has a habit of returning with ecstatic dance movements. To dance is to go on pilgrimage, and people dance more in periods of distress. During the French Revolution Paris went on one of the greatest dancing sprees in history.

Agonistic games are also pilgrimages. The word for chess player in Sanskrit is the same for pilgrim, 'he who reaches the opposite shore'. Footballers are little aware that they too are pilgrims. The ball they boot symbolises a migrant bird.

All our activities are linked to the idea of journeys. And I like to think that our brains have an information system giving us our orders for the road, and that here lie the mainsprings of our restlessness. At an early stage man found he could spill out all this information in one go, by tampering with the chemistry of the brain. He could fly off on an illusory journey or an imaginary ascent. Consequently settlers naïvely identified God with the vine, hashish or a hallucinatory mushroom, but true wanderers rarely fell prey to this illusion. Drugs are vehicles for people who have forgotten how to walk.

Actual journeys are more effective, economic and instructive than faked ones. We should tread the steps of Hesiod up Mount Helicon and hear the Muses. They are certain to appear if we listen carefully. We should follow the Taoist sages, Han Shan up Cold Mountain in his little hut, watching the seasons go by, or the great Li Po – 'You asked me what is my reason for lodging in the grey hills: I smiled but made no reply for my thoughts were idling on their own; like the flowers of the peach tree, they had sauntered off to other climes, to other lands that are not of the world of men.'

1970

IV

REVIEWS

ABEL THE NOMAD[1]

Wilfred Thesiger's *Arabian Sands* and *The Marsh Arabs* are classics in line with Doughty's *Travels in Arabia Deserta*. Yet his new autobiographical sketch, *Desert, Marsh and Mountain*, though it borrows large chunks of the two earlier books, is more absorbing than either. The subtitle, 'The World of a Nomad', gives a clue about what he is up to. The nomad in question is Mr Thesiger himself, as he travels, by camel or on foot, in Africa or in Asia, among tribesmen who are – or were – for the most part nomadic. At first sight, the book appears to be a collection of short travel-pieces, illustrated with photographs by someone with an unerring sense of composition. A closer look reveals a declaration of faith that goes a long way towards explaining the 'strange compulsion' which drives men like Wilfred Thesiger to seek, and find, the consolation of the desert.

He was born to travel. His father was British Minister in Addis Ababa. His first memories were 'of camels and of tents, of a river and men with spears'. His book was *Jock of the Bushveld*, that child's bible of the British Empire. His friends were orderlies and grooms who took him out hunting or held his pony. He was always a stranger among his own – as remote from his schoolfellows as he was from the few of his countrymen, such as the late Gavin Maxwell, who had the stamina to follow him on his journeys. A

[1] *Desert, Marsh and Mountain*, Wilfred Thesiger, London: Collins, 1979.

photograph taken at Eton shows a face already set in the mould of the horizon-struck dreamer.

He went back to Ethiopia in 1930 for the coronation of Haile Selassie. Afterwards, he made a journey across the country of the Danakils, first cousins of Kipling's 'fuzzy-wuzzies' and incredibly fierce. He found 'even more than I had dreamed of as a boy poring over *Jock of the Bushveld*', and, incidentally, crossed the tracks of Arthur Rimbaud, who had trekked up and down those '*routes horribles*' forty years before. The Danakil journey set the pattern for a life that turned into a perpetual tramp through the wilderness: an officer in the Sudan Political Service; in the Empty Quarter; in the Marshes of Southern Iraq; on the spring migration of the Bakhtiari; with the Kurds of the Zagros or the Kaffirs of the Hindu Kush; watching Nasser's planes bomb the Yemini Royalists; or living, as he now does, in a tent, shooting the odd buck for food, among the Samburu cattle-herdsmen of Northern Kenya.

Mr Thesiger makes no secret of his conviction that the heroic world of pastoral nomads is finer – morally and physically – than the life of settled civilisations: 'All that is best in the Arabs came from the desert.' (Indeed, the word *arab* means a 'dweller in tents', as opposed to *hazar* 'a man who lives in a house' – with the original implication that the latter was rather less than human.) It is, therefore, nothing short of catastrophic for him to find his old Bedu friends driving about in cars and seduced by the 'tawdriest and most trivial aspects of Western civilisation'. Of the Rashid tribe, his companions in the Empty Quarter, he writes: 'They wore their clothes with distinction, even if they were in rags. They were small deft men, alert and watchful, tempered in the furnace of the desert and trained to unbelievable endurance … They were fine-drawn and highly strung as thoroughbreds.'

These are not the reveries of an armchair anthropologist: Mr Thesiger knows what he is talking about. Time and again, he gives examples of Bedu courage, loyalty, generosity, open-mindedness;

and he contrasts these qualities with the narrow, close-fisted fanaticism of the oases-dwellers. It is the test of his stature as a writer that he can describe without a trace of embarrassment or sentimentality the rewards of winning the friendship of his two young guides, bin Kabina and bin Ghabaisha. He is not the confessional type. Yet when another friend, Falih bin Majid, gets killed in a shooting accident in the Marshes, he manages to inject, into a few terse lines, a pain made even more harrowing by his own inability to cry. The description of Falih's mourning father is equally fine: 'Majid, grey and unshaven, his great stomach bulging out in front of him, looked very tired, an old broken man filled with bitterness. "Why did it have to be Falih? Why Falih?" he burst out. "God, now I have no one left."'

Mr Thesiger has so absorbed the temper of the heroic world that his descriptions of raids, blood-feuds and reconciliations give his prose the character of an ancient epic or saga. Even plodding passages, full of what E. M. Forster called 'those dreadful Oriental names', will suddenly break into images of great beauty that suggest far more than they state: 'The sun was on the desert rim, a red ball without heat'; 'The wind blew cold off dark water and I heard waves lapping on an unseen shore.' For its internal rhythms and the cadence of its repetitions, this description of an Eden in the Western Hejaz should perhaps be read aloud:

We climbed steep passes where baboons barked at us from the cliffs and lammergeyer sailed over the misty depths, and we rested beside cold streams in forests of juniper and wild olive. There were wild flowers here, jasmine and honeysuckle, roses, pinks and primulas. Sometimes we spent the night in a castle with an amir, sometimes in a mud cabin with a slave, and everywhere we were well received. We fed well and slept in comfort, but I could not forget the desert and the challenge of the Sands.

An 'ache' to return to the desert is the constant theme of the book. It is easy to mock Mr Thesiger, as some have done, as an old-fashioned English eccentric who has wilfully romanticised the desert creed, or to complain that nomads have added nothing to art, to architecture, or the general glories of civilisation. But the origins of civilisation are not all that respectable. Pharaoh built the pyramid with slave-labour. Moses took his people back into the clean air of the desert and lived in a black tent, and when he died, he walked out of the camp and the vultures got him in a valley in Beth-Peor – 'and no man knoweth his tomb'. Mr Thesiger's beliefs are not eccentric. They are consistent with principles laid down, at one time or other since the beginning of civilisation, by historians, philosophers, poets, teachers and mystics. One strain of the Old Testament, particularly strong among the later prophets, harps on the theme that, by settling the Land instead of migrating through it, the Children of Israel have 'waxed fat and gone a-whoring' and will find favour with their God only when they go back to the black tents: 'And again I will make you live in tents as in the days of old' (Hosea, 12). *Desert, Marsh and Mountain* can, in fact, be read as a sustained lament for Abel the nomad, murdered by Cain, the planter and builder of the First City, whose sacrifice was unacceptable to the Lord, yet who would have dominion over his brother.

The most concise statement ever made on the nomad question comes from no less a historian than Ibn Khaldun: 'Nomads are closer to the created world of God and removed from the blameworthy customs that have infected the hearts of settlers.' Only they would avoid the cycles of decadence that have ruined every known civilisation – and, indeed, the nomad world has not changed since Abraham the Bedu sheikh went on journeys 'from the south even unto Bethel, unto the place where his tent had been at the beginning'.

There is a case for supposing that all the transcendental religions are stratagems for peoples whose lives were wrecked by settlement. But it is the paradox of Islam that, though the Hadj or Sacred Pilgrimage to Mecca reproduces for townspeople the automatic asceticism of desert life, and though the Fast of Ramadan was originally 'the month of burning', the real Bedu often have only the vaguest notions of religion and are shamelessly materialistic. As a Bedu told Palgrave in the last century, 'we will go up to God and salute him, and if he proves hospitable, we will stay with him: if otherwise, we will mount our horses and ride off.'

Nomads may be closer to the created world of God, but they are not a part of it. A nomad proper is a herdsman who moves his property through a sequence of pastures. He is tied to a most rigorous time-table and committed to the increase of his herds and his sons. It is no accident that such words as 'stock', 'capital', 'pecuniary' and even 'sterling' come from the pastoral world. And it is the nomad's fatal yearning for increase that causes the endless round of raid and feud, and finally tempts him to succumb to settlement.

By these standards, Mr Thesiger is not a nomad but a traveller, in whom the old sense of travel as 'travail' has been revived: at one point he writes that the cartilages in his knee wore out and he had to have them removed. There are no metaphysical overtones in his book: he is always the English gentleman explorer. Yet the form of asceticism he has practised over fifty years puts him in the class of other travellers – the Desert Fathers, the Irish Pilgrims, the fakirs, the Holy Wanderers of India, or marvellous intellects like the poet Li Po who travelled to discover the 'great calm' that is perhaps the same as the Peace of God.

It was said of the Buddha that he 'found the Ancient Way and followed it', and that his last words to his disciples were: 'Walk on!' It is not unreasonable to suppose that the first men walked long journeys through the wilderness of thorns and cutting grasses south of the Sahara: Mr Thesiger, it seems, has returned to the centre.

1979

THE ANARCHISTS OF
PATAGONIA[1]

In 1920 an anarchist revolution, called in the names of Proudhon,
Bakunin, Kropotkin and Malatesta, broke over the British-run
sheep farms of Southern Patagonia. Its instigator was a lanky
Gallician of twenty-three called Antonio Soto. He had chestnut
hair and a thrilling voice and was slightly wall-eyed; he had been
piously brought up by maiden aunts at El Ferrol, where he was a
contemporary of Francisco Franco. At seventeen he read Tolstoy's condemnation of military service, skipped to Argentina to
avoid his own, and drifted into the theatre and the fringes of the
anarchist movement.

Employed as a scene shifter in a travelling Spanish theatre
company, Soto ended up in Río Gallegos, a dismal seaport near
the Straits of Magellan. Here a compatriot told him of the plight of
the migrant farm workers, mostly mestizo Indians from the green
but over-populated island of Chiloe. The situation appealed to
Soto's messianic impulses. He switched from the theatre into
politics, got himself elected secretary-general of the local workers'
union and, with a crew of amateur revolutionaries, led his
followers to loot and burn, and finally left them to the firing
squads.

Osvaldo Bayer is a left-wing Argentine historian of German

[1] *Los Vengadores de la Patagonia Trágica*, Osvaldo Bayer, Buenos Aíres: Editorial Galerna,
1972–4.

descent. The facts speak for themselves; and the author is a brave man who has risked his life to publish them. The revolution of 1920–21 does indeed read like a prophecy of contemporary events in Chile and Argentina, though it must be said that Bayer's lapses into rhetoric and his polemical outbursts aimed at current military and foreign intervention in Latin America rather weaken the force of his narrative.

Patagonia, the backdrop to this story, is the wind-blown tip of the continent below latitude 42°, and is split between Chile and Argentina. The Chilean coasts are choked with rain forest, but east of the Andes there are deserts of grey-green thornscrub and grassy pampas that remind one of Nevada or Wyoming. After 1900, Patagonia actually became an extension of the rough-riding West: Butch Cassidy and the Sundance Kid came down and robbed the Bank of Tarapaca and London in Río Gallegos in 1905.

Magellan gave the name 'Patagon' to the Tehuelche Indian giant he saw dancing on the shore at St Julian in 1520. The word is supposed to mean 'Big-Foot' for the size of his moccasins, but this is not the case. The Tehuelches wore dog-head battle masks, and the Grand Patagon is a dog-headed monster in the chivalric romance *Primaleon of Greece* printed in Spain seven years before Magellan sailed. (Hence Caliban, who invoked the Tehuelche god Setebos, has additional claims to Patagonian ancestry – *vide* Trinculo's: 'I shall laugh myself to death at this puppy-headed monster.') The Tehuelches were guanaco hunters, whose size and booming voices belied their docile character. And after the sheep-farmers came, they died out – from drink, despair, disease and intermarriage.

Darwin had written of Patagonia: 'The curse of sterility is on the land', and for most of the nineteenth century Argentina had ignored it. There were a few Argentine settlements down the coast, but most of the colonising was Chilean. Chile occupied the Straits of Magellan in 1843, one day ahead of the French, and by the late 1870s her convict station at Punta Arenas had grown into a thriving port. Then Argentina woke up, realising that Darwin's estimate was ill-judged and, as the price of her neutrality while her neighbour was at war with Peru, forced a division of Patagonia roughly along the watershed of the Andes. The Chileans felt they had been tricked out of the best land and always looked for opportunities to get it back.

Meanwhile, an English resident of Punta Arenas brought the first sheep over from the Falklands in 1877. When they multiplied, others took the hint. The two big pioneers were a charmless Asturian, José Menéndez, and his son-in-law, Moritz Braun, the son of a Jewish butcher from the Baltic. Between them, the Braun and Menéndez families got colossal land grants from the Argentine Government, throttled the territory with their company, La Anonima, and imported stud flocks from New Zealand, farm-managers from the British army, and shepherds from the Highlands.

They became immensely rich. When he died in 1918 Don José left the surplus of his millions to Alfonso XIII of Spain. In Punta Arenas you can still see the Palais Braun, imported piecemeal from France in 1902, where, in a setting of damasks, Cordoba leathers, hygienic marbles, and a painting of amorous geese by Picasso's father, the Edwardian era has survived the Allende regime.

Other foreigners also got land in Patagonia. The Land Department in Buenos Aires deliberately favoured Anglo-Saxons, since they were identified with Progress, and such Argentine proprietors as there were tended to install British managers. The result was that Santa Cruz province looked like an outpost of the Empire administered by Spanish-speaking officials. Some of the British farms were – and still are – run by big outfits, quoted on the London Stock Exchange. But many settlers were 'kelpers' from the Falklands, with memories of the Highland clearances and nowhere else to go. Their estancias, though almost bankrupt, are still smartly painted up and remind one of an English boys' boarding school: the headmaster's house sits with its herbaceous borders, lawn-sprayers and bound copies of *Punch* and *Blackwood's*, while the peons sleep in spartan dormitories, have their orders posted on blackboards and make trivial purchases in the farm shop.

Bayer is not quite fair to the *latifundistas*. They had laboured for twenty-five years, and their position was still extremely precarious; what one government gave, another might take back without compensation so the temptation to get money out was irresistible. Because of their cheap labour force, Patagonian sheep-farmers had been able to undercut their Australian and New Zealand competitors and throughout the 1914–18 War there was a boom, but in the slump that followed there came new taxes, inflation, customs controls and workers' agitation. The farmers of Santa Cruz began to compare themselves with Russian aristocrats stranded on the steppe at the mercy of violent peasants.

One issue of the *Magellan Times*, the local English newspaper, carries a picture of a Russian country house, its owner grovelling to a slab-sided muscleman, with the caption: 'A nocturnal orgy of the Maximalists at the estate of Kislodovsk. 5,000 roubles or your lives!' Alongside an advertisement for 'party frocks by Marcells in beige georgette with a silver sash' was a profile of Trotsky, 'a sullen despot in the style of Nero, opening his murderous dispatches with a gold paper knife that once belonged to the Tsars ... note the sullen indifference with which he treats beautiful linen table cloths'.

The peons were almost all from Chiloe. They were tougher and poorer than the sun-loving Argentines and worked harder for less. Besides which, their employers could dump trouble-makers over the border and earn the approval of the authorities, who saw in the large numbers of Chilean nationals a threat to Argentine security. Bayer describes the Chilotes thus:

All day on horseback; their backsides calloused; in heat and cold; without women; without children, books or schooling. Always wearing the same submissive smile; always the clumsy evasiveness of the Chilean peon. Men with skins the colour of those who never wash. Numberless men with glassy stares. Men repressed, looking as if capon flesh were incarnate in their lifeless faces, in their bodies without beauty, in clothes fit only to cover their nakedness, not to keep out the cold ...

But this picture of the Chilotes as mindless victims of foreign greed does scant justice to their own culture, for the folklore of these steel-hard people is full of hellish visions of the outside world and prophesies a time when they will sweep the land of their oppressors. Like other pinioned races, their reserve will suddenly break down in bouts of sex, drink and violence (and did so before the coming of the Spaniards). This aspect of their character is something Bayer has overlooked.

Río Gallegos in 1920 was a grid of streets lined with corrugated iron buildings, with the smoke-stacks of the Swift Corporation's freezing-plant rearing above the prison yard. Antonio Soto had found a mentor, a bald and dandified Spanish lawyer, José Maria Borrero, who had left the University of Santiago de Compostela with a doctorate in theology and drifted to the end of the world where he ran a bi-weekly newspaper, *La Verdad*, and laid into the Anglo-Saxon plutocracy. His language thrilled his compatriots and they began to imitate his style: 'In this society of Judases and Pulchinellas Borrero alone preserves the rare integrity of man ... among these egotistic gluttons of lucre ... these twittering pachyderms with their snapping teeth and castrated consciences.'

Borrero introduced Soto to the local judge, Ismael Viñas, a youngish demagogue who also hated the foreign pirates and had done his best to ruin a Scottish sheep-farming company that had contravened the Argentine fisc. The trio formed an alliance against the landowners, hoteliers and general traders, and against two men in particular. One was the Acting-Governor of Santa Cruz, Edelmiro Correa Falcón, a tweedy anglophile and property agent, the chairman of the local Sociedad Rural. The other was Ibon Noya, the Spanish owner of the Buick garage and president of the Río Gallegos branch of the Argentine Patriotic League, a right-wing organisation formed to combat the bacillus of foreign ideology. In the case of Correa Falcón it was a case of love turned to hate; Judge Viñas had insulted the Acting-Governor's wife by appearing at a civic function on the arm of his concubine.

In September Soto began his career as a revolutionist by organising a strike of waiters at the Grand Hotel. The police chief of Río Gallegos was a big, bad-tempered Scot called Ritchie whose immediate reaction was to put all the rabble-rousers in jail. By the time he awoke to the real threat of a General Strike and the pitiful size of his own force, the Judge had already ordered the prisoners' release, but the strike spread and paralysed some estancias which were in the middle of lambing.

Soto then hoisted his political colours, the red and the black of anarchism. His next move, touching but not entirely to the point, was a march of Chilotes to commemorate the eleventh anniversary of the shooting of the Catalan educator Francisco Ferrer. Soto insisted that the workers were honouring Ferrer, as Catholics honoured the Maid of Orléans, or the Mohammedans Mohammed, but the police chief banned the demonstration, giving Viñas a chance to ridicule his ignorance of Ferrer's place in the history of ideas. The Judge squashed the ban and the march went ahead.

By the last week in October, the *Magellan Times* was giving gloomy warnings of the unrest. On the night of 1 November Soto escaped murder at the hands of a hired Chilean – the knife blade hit the silver watch in his waistcoat. Convinced of his mission, Soto called a general strike and marshalled a list of minimum demands for estancia workers. The tone of the document was quite sedate. Borrero and the Judge wanted only to rout the other faction, not to topple the system. But Soto insisted on a final clause: that his own Federación Obrera should mediate all disputes between employers and their men and concluded with a barrage of insults against the landowners and their system that 'placed the value of a man alongside that of a mule, a sheep or a horse'. The farmers offered better wages and conditions but would not let the chorus-boy step between them and their men. As they hoped, their offer produced a schism among the workers: Soto and the anarchists rejected the terms; the syndicalists accepted them, speaking of Soto's 'mental obtuseness and total ignorance of how to run a strike'. Soto replied that the syndicalists were pimps for the local brothel, La Chocolatería.

Isolated from the moderates, he then took up with some 'propagandists by the deed', who called themselves the Red Council and wore red armbands. The leaders were two Italians, one known as the '68' who had once made shepherdesses in a Dresden porcelain factory and the other a red-bearded army deserter called El Toscano. Their followers were a fluid mixture of German *Wandervögel*, Russian anarchists, two Scots, some North American cowboy-outlaws, and the usual corps of Chilotes.

At the head of up to five hundred rough-riders, the Red Council swooped on isolated farms, burning, requisitioning firearms, provisions and liquor, and taking the owners and managers hostage. The centre of their operations were the steppes east of Lago Argentino within easy reach of the Cordillera. In Río Gallegos Commissioner Ritchie sent his sub-commissioner Micheri to size up the situation. Also in the party were sergeant Sosa 'the Peon-Beater' and Jorge Pérez Millán Témperley, a pretty upper-class boy with a weakness for uniforms, who had joined the Gendarmería as a subaltern.

Over Christmas Micheri's party patrolled the lake and beat up peons at random, then retreated back across the pampas in two Ford cars. Passing the hotel of El Cerrito they fell into a Red Council ambush. Two policemen and a chauffeur were killed, the sub-commissioner was wounded, and Témperley was shot in the genitals.

Soto went into hiding and Borrero went to jail. When he came out he found that Ritchie had raided the offices of *La Verdad* and destroyed the typeface. In Buenos Aires, President Hipólito Yrigoyen received a firm note from the British Embassy and decided to send in the troops. His choice fell on a small but patriotic officer, Lieutenant Colonel Héctor Benigno Varela.

With the tenth Argentine Cavalry there sailed Captain Ignacio Yza, the appointed Governor of Santa Cruz, who had done everything to delay taking up his appointment. He was a radical but knew nothing about Patagonia. He and Varela took the strikers' part against the foreign land-sharks, dismissed Ritchie, ignoring the warnings of Correa Falcón, and offered free pardons to all who surrendered their arms. The Red Council were suspicious but, in the best anarchist tradition, allowed themselves to be overruled.

Soto came out of hiding and claimed a total victory over the army, private property and the State. 'You'll see,' Ibon Noya told Varela. 'Once you go this will start up again.' 'If it starts up again,' the Colonel said, 'I'll come back and shoot them by dozens.'

Noya was right. Soto was puffed up with success and made the Governor's life impossible. He tried to organise a strike in the Swift freezer, but the new police chief outwitted him and herded the workers back into the factory. As winter closed in, Soto went to Buenos Aires to canvass for support at the eleventh Workers' Congress, but the professionals bickered over the policies of Lenin and Zinoviev and ignored the Patagonian delegate. Meanwhile the coastal towns of Patagonia were convulsed with arson, sabotage and at least one murder. By spring, Soto was dreaming of a revolt that would spread up from Patagonia and engulf the country. He had three lieutenants – a Bakuninist ex-waiter called Outerelo; a Syndicalist official, Albino Arguëlles; and a courteous and silent gaucho called Facón Grande for the size of his knife. Dr Borrero was conspicuous by his absence. The wreck of *La Verdad* had silenced him and he saw the dangers of provoking the army a second time. Besides, he was having an affair with an estanciero's daughter and had taken advantage of depressed land prices to buy a little place of his own. Then it was discovered that he had, all along, been on the payroll of the Brauns and Menéndezes; the anarchist broadsheets spoke of Judas' thirty pieces of silver.

The Red Council began the second phase of the revolution on their own, but were betrayed to the police and bundled off to jail. Soto should have taken the hint, but he still believed the government was neutral, and sent 'evangelists of Bakunin' round the sheep farms giving orders to raid and take hostages. On the whole the prisoners were well-treated, but a Mr Robbins of Torquay cut his throat in a fit of depression.

President Yrigoyen called Varela a second time and told him to use whatever measures were necessary. The *Magellan Times* commented: 'So far the Argentine Cavalry has done nothing to justify its presence, but we hope that Commandante Varela is preparing a campaign that will completely stamp out this revolt and that the bandits will receive a lesson they will not forget for a good number of years.'

This time Varela had indeed come 'not to pardon but to clean'. (He used the words *limpiar* and *depurar*.) He interpreted his instructions as tacit permission for a bloodbath, but since Congress had just abolished the death penalty, he had to inflate Soto's Chilotes to 'military forces perfectly armed and better munitioned ... enemies of the country in which they live'. Many, it was claimed, were salitreros from the nitrate mines in northern Chile;

when three Chilean carabineers were captured inside the frontier, this was evidence that the Chilean government lay behind the revolt; a Russian Menshevik with a notebook of Cyrillic characters plainly signified the red hand of Moscow. (Bayer categorically denies Chile's involvement, though members of the Argentine Frontier Commission assured me that documents exist to the contrary.)

The ill-armed strikers melted away before the troops. Varela filed reports of stirring gunfights and arsenals captured, but the *Magellan Times* for once told the truth: 'Various bands of rebels, finding their cause lost, have surrendered and the bad element among them have been shot.'

The army's performance was one of outstanding cowardice. On five occasions the soldiers got the peons to surrender by promising to respect their lives. Each time the killings began straight afterwards: they were shot into graves they dug themselves or their corpses burned on bonfires of thornscrub. Borrero made an exaggerated estimate of 1,500 in his book *La Patagonia Trágica*, but the number of the dead is uncertain. Officially the firing squads did not exist.

Soto's megalomaniac dream finally collapsed at La Anita, the prize Menéndez estancia, ringed by snowy mountains, with a view of the Moreno Glacier sliding through black forests into a turquoise lake. Here, with five hundred men, he held his hostages in the big green and white house with its *art nouveau* conservatory. When he heard of the massacres on the plain, and of Captain Viñas Ibarra's column not far up the valley, he knew his number was up. His character became more frigid and austere, while his talk of the dignity of man more than ever obscured any understanding of real men. At nights he went off to sleep alone, and the Chilotes, who required their leaders to share every detail of their lives, began to loathe him. At his last conference, the hardliners, led by two Germans, wanted to barricade the shearing shed with wool bales and fight to the last man, but Soto said he was not dog meat, he would run for it and continue the revolution elsewhere. And the Chilotes preferred to trust even the Argentine army rather than Soto's promises.

Soto sent two peons to Viñas Ibarra to ask for terms. 'Terms for what?' he asked and told them to make terms with Jesus Christ. Subsequently, he demanded an unconditional surrender, but said he would spare their lives. That night Soto and a few others rode out over the Cordillera and escaped into Chile. (He died at Punta Arenas in the 1960s, filled with remorse, the proprietor of a small restaurant run on anarchist principles.) In the morning the soldiers freed the hostages and herded the peons into the shearing shed. One of the hostages, who had been a professional Indian killer, said he wanted thirty-seven corpses for his thirty-seven stolen horses. The three hundred Chilotes thought they would be expelled over the border into Chile. But at seven in the morning the door of the shed opened and a sergeant ostentatiously distributed picks to a work-party. The others heard them marching off and then the chink of picks on stone. 'They're digging graves,' they said. The door opened again at eleven and the men were led out in groups for the estancieros to pick out the men they wanted back at work. It was just like sorting sheep.

The unwanted ones – mouths lowered and eyes distended – were led off past the sheep-dip and round a scrubby hill. From the yard the others heard the crackle of shots and saw turkey buzzards soaring in from the mountains. About 120 men died that day. One of the executioners said, 'They went to their deaths with a passivity that was truly astonishing.'

The British community was overjoyed. The *Magellan Times* praised Varela's 'splendid courage, running about the firing line as though on parade ... Patagonians should take their hats off to the tenth Argentine Cavalry, these very gallant gentlemen'. Ibon Noya's Patriotic League was already urging Varela's appointment as Governor. At a luncheon, Noya spoke of the 'sweet emotion of these moments' and of his 'satisfaction mixed with gratitude at being rid of the plague'. The colonel replied modestly that he had only done his duty as a soldier, and the twenty British present, being men of few Spanish words, broke into song: 'For he's a jolly good fellow ...'

In Buenos Aires it was a different story. There was no hero's welcome for Varela, only graffiti reading: 'SHOOT THE CANNIBAL OF THE SOUTH!' Few left-wingers cared too much about Soto or the Chilotes, but the army had, unwittingly, killed a Syndicalist official and Congress was in uproar. Yrigoyen appointed Varela director of a cavalry school and hoped the crisis would simmer down. But at dawn on 27 January 1923, as Varela was on his way to work, he was approached by a a tall, red-haired man in a dark suit carrying a copy of the *Deutsche La Plata Zeitung* and a bomb. As the bomb exploded, the assassin fired his Colt twice and pierced Varela's jugular. 'I have revenged my brothers,' he mumbled in bad Spanish as he fell, 'I do not need to live.'

The killer was Kurt Wilkens, a thirty-six-year-old German wanderer from Schleswig-Holstein, who had been a miner and anarchist in the United States until the immigration authorities expelled him. In Buenos Aires he washed cars by day and read great books by night. In his lodgings police found framed photos of Tolstoy and Kropotkin, and copies of Goethe's *Werther* and Knut Hamsun's *Hunger*. He claimed to have made the bomb himself, but there were no traces and the police were sceptical.

One of the mourner's at Varela's funeral was an effeminate young man who moped round the coffin, sobbing and swearing revenge. The murderer, who had recovered, was put in the Prison of the Encausaderos ('those awaiting trial'). Wilken's new warder was strangely nervous; he paced up and down in the hot sticky night until his spell was over, then he entered the cell, rubbed the barrel of his Mauser against the German's shoulder blades, asked him, 'Are you Wilkens?' 'Jawohl,' came the answer, and he fired. The young warder rushed to his superior and said, 'I have avenged the death of my cousin, Colonel Varela.'

The warder, the same boy who behaved so strangely at Varela's funeral, was Jorge Pérez Millán Témperley, last seen at El Cerrito and now permanently unhinged by the wound to his genitals. How he became Wilken's warder was never explained, for the inquiry smoothed the issues over. He got off with a light sentence, eight years, in view of his 'physical abnormality' and was soon transferred to a hospital for the criminally insane.

One of his fellow internees was a Yugoslav midget, a compulsive talker who had once murdered his doctor. On Monday afternoon, 9 February 1925, Témperley, in a black mood, was writing a letter to the National President of the Argentine Patriotic League, when Lukič, the Yugoslav, poked his head round the door of the cubicle, shouted, 'This is for Wilkens!' and shot him.

The mechanics of vengeance had taken their final turn. The question was: Who gave Lukič the gun? The police eventually pinned this on another internee, Boris Vladimirovič, a Russian of some pedigree, a biologist, artist and revolutionary writer who had lived in Switzerland and known Lenin. After the 1905 revolution he took to drink and then went to Argentina to begin again on a cattle ranch in Santa Fé. But the old life drew him back. In 1919 he bungled the robbery of a bureau de change in Buenos Aires to raise funds for an anarchist publication. A man was killed and Vladimirovič got twenty-five years in Ushuaia, Tierra del Fuego, the prison at the end of the world. But the cold, the clouds and black water drove him mad. He sang the songs of the Motherland, and for the sake of quiet, the Governor had him transferred to hospital in the capital. That Sunday visiting day, two Russian friends brought him a revolver in a basket of fruit. The case was hard to prove, and there was no trial. But Boris

Vladimirovič disappeared for ever, paralysed, into the House of the Dead.

Last year, I met near Punta Arenas an old Chilote sheep shearer who had escaped the massacre and had known Antonio Soto. His hands were knotted with arthritis, and he sat wearing a beret huddled over a wood stove. When I asked about the Revolution he said, 'The army had permission to kill everybody' – as if one could hope for nothing else. But when he talked of Soto and the leaders, he shook, and, as if surprised by the violence of his own voice, shouted, 'They were not workers. They never worked a day in their lives. Barkeepers! Hairdressers! Acrobats! *Artistas!*'

1976

THE ROAD TO THE ISLES[1]

No biographer should embark on Robert Louis Stevenson without taking stock of the effect of Edinburgh on its inhabitants. For the gaunt northern capital demands from them, and usually gets, a very specific moral commitment. Stevenson was an Edinburgh phenomenon; his childhood in the city set up a repetitious see-saw of attraction and loathing that almost predetermined his death in the South Seas. Coddled in the sickroom by masterful women, he turned in boyish fantasy to all-male adventures in bright islands in the sun. Once installed in Samoa, in the style of a laird, with his family and the solid furniture of his father's house about him, he finally grew up and came to terms with the 'precipitous city' he had once hated to the backbone.

The late James Pope-Hennessy's book makes interesting reading. He has picked over the abundant documentation, assembled at the turn of the century by people who turned the commemoration of Stevenson into a literary industry, and he has selected well, packing the story with telling detail and anecdote. He gives a straightforward account of Stevenson's placid, cheerful mother, from whom he inherited his weak chest; of his morose and pious father, the lighthouse engineer; and of his nurse, the fearsome Alison Cunningham, who whipped his imagination into a frenzy of religious torment. He dwells on his sexless love affair

[1] *Robert Louis Stevenson*, James Pope-Hennessy, London: Jonathan Cape, 1974.

with the Madonna-like Mrs Sitwell, and goes over the vicissitudes of his bizarre marriage with the American Fanny Osbourne. We are given a vivid glimpse of artistic, expatriate bohemia at Grez in the Forest of Fontainebleau. We also get something of the essential perversity of Stevenson's character, of his hysterical gaiety in the face of fatal illness, and of his gift of making himself irresistible to both sexes.

And yet Pope-Hennessy leaves the impression he was bored by Stevenson, both as a writer and as a man. The Stevenson family and its entourage glide through the book, picturesque figures in a picturesque decor, but there is little to indicate why they function as they do – until, that is, they board the yacht *Casco* and sail for the South Seas. At this point they enter Pope-Hennessy's own orbit of interest, and the reader's interest quickens in turn. He plainly enjoyed visiting Samoa; and we enjoy his descriptions of its luxuriance, its warmth and colour, and the pale, glistening bodies of the natives. In an earlier book, *Verandah*, he wrote brilliantly about his grandfather's governorship of Mauritius. He should perhaps have expanded the last seventy-odd pages of this one, and used the Stevensons as a peg to illustrate the pleasures and delusions of Europeans who settle in a tropical island paradise.

Pope-Hennessy did not set out to write a critical biography of Stevenson or to treat his books as more than so many incidents in his career. This is a pity, especially with so autobiographical a writer. Stevenson was profoundly self-centred and had a morbid concern for his public image. He liked to think he was free with information about himself. In fact he kept tight rein on the confessional; but, consciously or not, he was always dropping broad hints in his stories. Pope-Hennessy's decision to concentrate on the life and not the works is, however, excusable. Stevenson was a talented story-teller but he was never first-rate. His grasp of character was limited to a few stock types; overdrawn and larger than life. He was unduly concerned with the niceties of style, advising young writers to bow their heads before the idol of technique, but in his own case the result tends to be limp and ineffectual. He was also unable to write clearly about the present and drifted off into imaginary fancy dress occasions. He is at his most enjoyable when writing for children, when he does not complicate the plot with tangential moral postures. But that is hardly the mark of a first-rate writer.

Nor can one think of his life as a first-rate performance. He was a careful man who lacked the open-hearted audacity of a Wilde. He was often on the verge of some splendid and dangerous act, but caution got the better of him. His vaunted revolt against Victorian propriety and his descent into low-life were half-hearted and tempered by fear of scandal. He was also something of a prig. He cultivated a reputation for womanising (without much evidence), yet he was always ready to weigh in against joyless lust. A vein of self-satisfied meanness overlaid his generosity; his hand-outs usually provoked resentment. His denial of faith was calculated to pain his Calvinist father, yet *Travels with a Donkey* tails off into an anti-Catholic, pro-Protestant tract. He harped on the need for the simple life, alone or out in the open with the woman one loves, only to cumber himself with the hefty trappings of the middle class. He yearned for adventure, for a 'pure dispassionate adventure such as befell the great explorers'. But he hadn't the stomach for it; on the whole, he travelled in a world made safe for aesthetes. He longed for a Great Man Friend, a fellow-adventurer like Queequeg in *Moby Dick*; in practice his chosen playmate was Fanny's son, Lloyd Osbourne, for whom he wrote *Treasure Island*. He claimed to suffer under the stultifying drowsiness of Victorian peace ('Shall we never shed blood? This prospect is too grey') – and spent much of his time playing with toy soldiers.

When he died at Vailima in Samoa in 1894, the British Empire was at its height. Stevenson, the champion of native causes, was hailed in some circles as a latter-day saint. Stevenson, the writer of boyish tales (in a world run by overgrown boys), was acclaimed as though he were one of the great novelists of all time. British and American readers pored admiringly over each perfect sentence. The first edition of *Treasure Island* acquired tremendous value among collectors. The young American bibliomane Harry Elkins Widener said he never travelled without his copy; it went down with him on the *Titanic*. Why such an obvious second-rater came to enjoy so inflated a reputation would make a very worthwhile subject, but again, Pope-Hennessy does not get us very far. Henry James, writing to commiserate with Fanny, was close to the mark: 'There have been – I think – for a man of letters, few deaths more romantically right.' Perhaps the Stevenson secret lay in the fact that he did (or appeared to do) the kind of things the public expects from its heroes. And he managed to attract a great deal of publicity for them. Whether his acts were genuine or faked is beside the point. The events of his life and the circumstance of his death have a mythic wholeness common to figures of heroic legend – a difficult childhood, an overbearing foster-mother, a revolt from the authority of the father, a journey to a far country, marriage to a stranger, a fight against menacing forces (in this case a tubercular chest), return and reconciliation with the father, public acclaim, and then a second departure followed by death in a remote and mysterious situation.

It is Stevenson's second-rateness that makes him interesting. His predicament is very familiar – the spoilt child of worthy, narrow-minded parents, unwilling to follow in the family business, longing to slough off civilisation in favour of healthy primitivism, yet tied to home by links of affection and cash, Stevenson is the forerunner of countless middle-class children who litter the world's beaches, or comfort themselves with anachronistic pursuits and worn-out religions. *Travels with a Donkey* is the prototype of the incompetent undergraduate voyage.

Edinburgh is the key to understanding Stevenson. Pope-Hennessy seems to have gone there as a tourist on a literary pilgrimage; he failed to take the measure of it, and missed some valuable clues. Edinburgh is a place of absolute contrast and paradox. A sense of quality in men and things goes hand in hand with chaotic squalor. The rational squares and terraces of the New Town confront the daunting skyline of the Old. Slums still abut the houses of the rich. Wild mountain scenery impinges on the heart of the city. On fine summer days nowhere is lighter and more airy; for most of the year there are icy blasts or a clammy sea fog, the *haar* of the east coast of Scotland. Edinburgh is contemptuous of the present. In no other city in the British Isles do you feel to the same extent the oppressive weight of the past. Mary Queen of Scots and John Knox are a presence. The dead seem more alive than the living. There is a claustrophobic, coffin-like atmosphere that makes Glasgow, in comparison, seem a paradise of life and laughter. Moderate health is virtually unknown. Either people enjoy robust appetites, or they are ailing and require protection. Heady passions simmer below the surface. In winter the city slumbers all week in blue-faced rectitude, only to explode on Saturday evenings in an orgy of drink and violence and sex. In some quarters the pious must pick their way to church along pavements spattered with vomit and broken bottles.

From his endless hours at the kirk Stevenson got the lecturing tone that creeps into his work. From his house in Heriot Row, he got his careful good taste; from Edinburgh conversation, his infuriating archaisms and refined, euphemistic circumlocutions; from the city's parades and martial music, his suppressed militarism; from its blood-stained legends, his fondness for the ghoulish. Under the influence of his training at the Edinburgh Bar, he makes his characters plead their cause, rather than state their case. Edinburgh, the historical stage-set, conditioned his rejection of Zola's realism and inspired his own rather fey romancing. The model for *Dr Jekyll and Mr Hyde* was a symbolic Edinburgh character of the eighteenth century, Deacon Brodie, a respectable cabinet-maker who was a thief in off-hours and eventually got himself hanged. Stevenson set *Dr Jekyll and Mr Hyde* in London, but it was Chesterton who spotted that it was an Edinburgh story, with its pattern of light and darkness, its rich mansion giving out on to a slum, its Calvinistic antithesis of absolute good and evil. It does not say much for Stevenson's understanding or tolerance that he should bestow his sympathies on Dr Jekyll and damn Mr Hyde.

From Edinburgh too came his compulsion to escape. Most of its citizens, at some time, are swept by the urge to get out. The young Stevenson recorded how he watched with longing the southbound trains leaving Waverley Station; and writing to his mother in 1874, he warned her not to mind his prolonged absences: 'You must remember that I shall be a nomad, more or less, until my days be done.' One side of Stevenson was the perennial boy with the pack on his back, always happier to be somewhere else, unable to face the complications of sex, and ready to work it off on a bike. He belongs, in spirit, to a long line of literary vagabonds; Whitman, Rimbaud and Hart Crane are other examples who come to mind. Stevenson undoubtedly derived a good deal of his glorification of the open road from Whitman, but he never achieved the vigour of the American's athletic outpourings.

The other side of Stevenson was the man with the staid, conventional view that he should marry and settle down. In a way his choice of a wife was ideal. Fanny Vandegrift Osbourne was another very familiar type – the tough, neurotic American, separated from her husband, approaching middle age yet still pretty, with children, in Europe, in search of the arts. She was a girl from the Midwest, married to her childhood sweetheart, who had grown from a beautiful boy into a philandering layabout. Fanny appears to have been very naïve about her husband's love affairs until they were thrust under her nose. She then developed a distaste for aggressive masculinity, and perhaps a distaste for sex in general. The tomboyish element in her character helped her survive the Nevada mining camps to which Sam Osbourne dragged her, but the rootless shiftings of her first marriage instilled in her a rapacious appetite for property and an obsession with minute social distinctions. The death of her younger son in Paris in 1876 turned her into a guilt-ridden woman with an urge to save someone or something. The young Scottish exquisite, who was chronically ill, awoke her salvationist impulses.

Pope-Hennessy reads the Stevenson marriage as a straight love story. In a sense he is right. There is every reason why the gauche, elfin lad, with his 'odd intense gaze', should have been drawn to an attractive older woman. Furthermore, any transatlantic love affair holds an extra fascination for both sides, combining the charm of the exotic with an ease of communication. It is fairly certain that Fanny and Louis became lovers at Grez. But there was not going to be much sex in this marriage, and I do not think Pope-Hennessy has plumbed its complexity. Fanny was to be the dominant partner. In good times, she was to be companion, fellow-adventurer, sister and mother, but hardly ever the lover. In bad times she was to be the devoted, iron-willed sick-nurse, filling the emotional gap left by Alison Cunningham: indeed, she seems to have preferred the role of nurse to all others.

In *Catriona*, which Stevenson wrote as a sequel to *Kidnapped*, there is one telling incident where the hero and heroine have to defend themselves. Catriona laments that she was not born a man-child and able to wield a sword, because David Balfour (a law student like Stevenson) had never learnt to use one. Some critics have suggested that Stevenson was impotent. There is even talk of a 'lasting injury' to his manhood, acquired from an Edinburgh whore. He himself was the first to say he did not want a family of his own, while it was only at the end of his writing career that he

brought himself to handle female characters. To introduce
women, he once said, was 'poison bad world for the romancer'.
There was in Stevenson a girlishness, always kept within the
bounds of Victorian prudery, that thrilled at tough, aggressive
masculinity. The sailors of *Treasure Island* are nut-brown and
soiled and scarred, and they foreshadow the Samoan house-boys
that, together with Lloyd Osbourne, he selected for their beauty at
Vailima. The novels are also filled with handsome greying
bachelors who take a 'fancy to the lady'. In the *Weir of Hermiston*
fragment, the young tentative Archie Weir (a self-portrait) says
goodbye to Lord Glenalmond, 'his eyes dwelling on those of his
old friend like those of a lover on his mistress's'. Stevenson is well
known to have had a father-fixation, and once spoke of his
excitement and horror at the beauty of his father stripped on the
beach at North Berwick.

This carrying-on has naturally led one particular kind of critic
to think the worst of Long John Silver's wooden leg. But
Stevenson was innocently amused by his own girlishness. When
the Italian portrait-painter Gugliemo Nerli came to Samoa and
painted him, he wrote the following scrap of doggerel:

> *Oh will he paint me the way I like,*
> *as bonny as a girlie,*
> *Or will he make me an ugly tyke,*
> *and be ... to Mr Nerli!*

Had he been a homosexual, or known what it was to be one, he
would surely not have written these arch and embarrassing lines.
Yet I do think we have to allow that part of Fanny's attraction was
her son Lloyd; and the fact that, on Louis's death, Lloyd all but
died of grief, makes it clear that their passionate friendship was far
from one-sided.

Louis loved Fanny desperately. He got it into his head that he would marry her, and he did. He could not live without her, and, on receiving a hysterical telegram from her, he pursued her to San Francisco. This was the critical moment of his life, and I do not think Pope-Hennessy has understood it. After an appalling journey on an emigrant ship and train, Louis arrived in California, battered, scabby, wheezing and probably near death. Fanny and Lloyd welcomed him with open arms, but something was wrong. She was having a nervous breakdown, brought on by her divorce, and she dithered over a union with an invalid now as penniless as herself. In despair Louis went off on one of his lonely hikes, collapsed and was saved from death by an old rancher. In the winter of 1879–80 he lived alone in squalid lodgings in Monterey and San Francisco, half-starving, wrecking his lungs from the sea-fog, and breaking himself with work. He refused offers of cash from his London friend Sidney Colvin, saying he saw this period as a test of endurance. Meanwhile Fanny held off; she lived in a cottage across the bay at Oakland and saw him perhaps twice a week. She did not even invite him for Christmas. On 26 December he wrote home: 'For four days I have spoken to no one, but my landlady or landlord or the waiters in the restaurant. This is not a gay way to pass Christmas and I must own the guts are a little knocked out of me.'

And the guts *were* knocked out of him. In the spring, Louis had his first haemorrhage from the lungs, and Fanny decided to marry him. The two events were simultaneous and connected. Unkind witnesses said that Fanny thought she was marrying a corpse and hoped to profit as Stevenson's widow. This is unfair. But it is hard to escape the conclusion that Louis courted death in San Francisco in order to qualify to be ill enough for Fanny to marry him. The marriage was based on the fact of his illness. Her well-being depended on his being flat on his back, on having him well enough to be dependent on her. Her protective streak, like that of Alison Cunningham, had a deadly side that would smother and unman him. Sargent's brilliant portrait of the pair, painted at Bournemouth, says it all – he, the pale, agitated narcissist, twiddling his moustachios and gazing into the mirror, she, a dumpy, sedentary figure in oriental costume. The Stevensons were in some ways a very modern couple.

But Fanny turned him into a writer. Always claiming second sight, she said she knew she was marrying a genius 'if he lives and works!' She used her flair for organisation to get him down to work and write money-making books. Had he remained well and single and lived in England, the chances are he would have struck, like his friend W. E. Henley, a mediocre figure with such talent as he had sucked dry in incestuous coteries. Fanny unscrupulously used the sickbed (his sheets were stained with ink and blood and gravy) and a series of sanatoria to protect Stevenson from his friends: and once they had moved to the South Seas, she could gloat with satisfaction over the fact that she had, at last, wheedled him out of the orbit of literary London.

Here she miscalculated. The South Pacific suited his health far better than she could have imagined. His lungs stopped bleeding. He now put on weight and muscle. He too became nut-brown and swam and did manual work. His ocean cruises, first on the yacht and then on rough copra schooners, toughened him and gave him confidence as a man. But she could not take it. After a rough passage to Hawaii, he wrote with evident pleasure: 'My wife is no great shakes. She is the one who has suffered most.' And, when they settled in Samoa and began building the house he continued to emerge from the cycle of unmanning prostration. He also mastered his fear of the opposite sex. At the time of his death he was creating, for the first time, two flesh-and-blood women – Kirstie and Christina Elliott in *Weir of Hermiston*.

But Louis's recovery drove Fanny frantic. She turned Vailima into emotional bedlam. She screamed and threw tantrums. They had to give her laudanum and even hold her down. Since she had lost absolute control over her husband, she launched into schemes for extending the house from a modest hide-out into a grandiose establishment. Her extravagance, combined with his Scottish fear of ruin, pressed him to earn more and more royalties. He reacted by cloistering himself with his step-daughter, the beautiful Belle Strong, who became his amanuensis and to whom he was evidently attracted. He became morose and pined for Scotland and then he cracked under the strain. The cerebral haemorrhage, which killed him, left Fanny free to play the role of martyr's widow. It was a role which suited her talent for drama, which she enjoyed, and from which she knew how to profit. The legend of 'RLS' was secure.

1974

VARIATIONS ON AN IDÉE FIXE[1]

Admirers of *King Solomon's Ring* and *Man Meets Dog* will be relieved that Konrad Lorenz has reverted to his earlier vein. His last two books must have been a bitter disappointment, even to those who accepted *On Aggression* as a work of oracular significance. One of them, entitled *Behind the Mirror*, purported to be a 'search for a Natural History of Human Knowledge', but was impenetrable to the non-academic reader. The other, *Civilised Man's Eight Deadly Sins*, was easy enough – a diatribe in the language of the world-saver that dragged out the musty metaphors of social Darwinism and could have been written in the late 30s. Overpopulation and the ruin of the landscape were galloping cancers. He inveighed against the inertia of public opinion; the universal mania for the new; the lack of courtship rituals that made for stable marriages; and he feared that our civilisation would fall to the less pampered peoples of the East.

The Year of the Greylag Goose, however, proves he has not lost his light touch or ability to charm. He presents the book as the record of four seasons spent studying his favourite bird in the 'fairytale surroundings' of Lake Alm in Austria. The result is extremely pretty and will doubtless beguile a wide audience, partly through

[1] *The Year of the Greylag Goose*, Konrad Lorenz, New York: Harcourt Brace Jovanovich, 1979.

the colour photographs of Sybille and Klaus Kalas, partly through Lorenz's special gift of getting under the skin of other creatures. The mountains are beautiful; the air is crystalline, and the greylag itself is a marvellous bird of muted greys and whites, with a beak the colour of red coral and slightly paler feet. On page after page exquisite images illustrate the flowers, the other animals of Lake Alm, and the geese themselves, courting, mating, nesting, hatching, fighting, swimming, moulting, flying, or feeding in the snow. On the last three spreads, a goose closes its eyelids and drifts into the deepest sleep.

Lorenz himself, in bathing shorts, sou'wester, or anorak, appears as the venerable, white-bearded naturalist, the Nobel Prize Winner who has never lost his capacity to marvel at the wonders of nature. When wild geese answer his call, he feels he has stepped back into a 'paradise of peaceful coexistence' with his fellow creatures. On the other hand, his knowledge of evolution has earned him the right to preach sermons that will be understood by anyone who takes the trouble to read between the lines. In the postscript, he hopes that the book 'will inspire overworked people who are alienated by nature with a sense of what is good and of their duty to protect and preserve nature's living things'.

Lorenz grew up at Altenberg on the Danube, and still lives in the fantastical neo-baroque mansion built by his father, a rich Viennese surgeon. His love affair with greylag geese began when he was a little boy watching them migrate down-river. By the age of six he had absorbed a popular account of Darwinism by Wilhelm Boelsche (through whose chief work, *Vom Bazillus zum Affenmenschen*, Hitler first latched onto the idea of evolution). He decided to become a palaeontologist and, in the garden, played at being an iguanadon with the girl who became his wife. Later, as a young scientist, he kept a flock of greylags in and around the house; and one of the funniest passages in *King Solomon's Ring* describes Lorenz Senior entertaining the geese to tea in his study, where they made messes on the Persian carpet. Frau Lorenz once asked a psychiatrist friend, 'What is this mania of Konrad's for geese?' 'It's a perversion,' he said. 'Same as any other.'

Lorenz has always been at pains to preface his books with avowals of scientific objectivity. At the start of *On Aggression*, he promised to lead his readers 'by the route which I took myself ... for reasons of principle. Inductive natural science always starts without preconceptions and proceeds from this to the abstract laws they all obey.' In the new book, the observer is the lens of the camera, 'the very symbol of objectivity'. Yet, though Lorenz claims to have written the text around the photographs, that doesn't stop him repeating the ingrained prejudices he has been hammering out for more than forty years, with the persistence of the Vicar of Bray.

His professional colleagues prefer to distinguish two Lorenzes. One is the 'Father of Ethology' (the book jacket calls him the 'Father of the Greylag Geese'), who pioneered the study of 'blocks' of genetically inherited behaviour in the vertebrates and contributed the valuable concept of 'imprinting'. The second Lorenz is the blustering philosopher-politician, whose argument from animals to man rests on rather shaky foundations. Yet his theses are so closely worked, and his career is so much of one piece, that I find it impossible to divide the Lorenzes.

His message is that all human behaviour is biologically determined: that when we speak of love, hate, anger, grief, ambition, loyalty, friendship, and so forth, we are speaking on precisely the same level as the ethologist who uses 'aggressivity', 'rank-order drive', 'male bonding', or 'territoriality' to describe the behaviour of other species. Once the 'drives', or appetites, of human beings are isolated, it will be possible to propose a biology of ethics that will supplant the half-truths of religion or secular morality. We are not free, but bound by evolutionary law. The function of reason is not to free us from our instinct, but to protect us from our own sins against nature. 'Animals', he writes in this book, 'do not *need* a sense of moral responsibility, since under natural conditions their inclinations lead them to what is *right*.' Man, however, is a domesticated species, whose innate schemes of behaviour have been blunted by the process of becoming human, and tend to get hopelessly brutalised in the conditions of the big modern city.

Now it happens that the family life of the greylag goose is an ideal mirror for Lorenz to show up the flaws of instinct in man. He quotes his father as saying: 'After the dog, the greylag goose is the most suitable animal for association with human beings.' In fact, he never tires of quoting his father as a reservoir of sound, old-fashioned common sense; and it must have been most reassuring for both to find that greylag society should conform to ideals of an upper-middle-class family in the late Austro-Hungarian Empire.

The geese are monogamous. They fall in love and stay in love. They have long courtship rituals that end in a kind of marriage ceremony. The ganders work off their aggressive drives in fights that establish a hierarchy of breeding. Defeated rivals go off alone, get depressed, and are liable to accidents. Sometimes a gander seduces another gander's goose and a divorce results. If one partner dies the survivor goes into mourning. Low-ranking geese look up to their elders and betters and stand around, as spectators, when the aristocrats fight. The whole goose colony drums up militant enthusiasm when threatened by an outside menace.

The hereditary principle is confirmed in that well-born goslings shoo off a grown-up commoner, providing they are on their own home ground. Sometimes two, and even three, ganders will form a homosexual bond, though none will consent to the passive role. These blood-brothers are stronger than 'any normal pair in courage and fighting strength', and 'always occupy a high rank in the social hierarchy'. It goes without saying that full-blooded greylags are superior – morally and physically – to the farmyard geese, whose services are sometimes enlisted at Lake Alm to hatch a clutch of eggs: 'These creatures, rendered stupid by many years of domestication, are incapable of reliable incubation: they have lost the well-defined instinctive behaviour patterns a wild goose exhibits.'

Lorenz shows no sign of abandoning his view of the Big City as a magnified barnyard that favours the selection of genetic deviants, whose unscrupulous behaviour is as repugnant as their stunted appearance. When I called on him a few years ago, he said, 'Since I have lived here at Altenberg, I have noticed a progressive *cochonification* of the boys swimming in the Danube. How would you say that in English? Porkification! Fat boys and fat men! The same in domesticated animals ... Complete unselectivity of feeding habits!'

'But surely', I said, 'that's the fault of the food manufacturers. It's not genetic.'

'I don't care if it's cultural devolution, or genetic devolution, I know cultural devolution moves ten times faster than genetic devolution. *But a culture behaves exactly like a species!*'

Now if you let Lorenz carry you any further with this argument, you might find yourself drawn to the conclusion that the finest specimens of humanity, 'the strong, manly men' he is always hoping for, have a duty to suppress the inferiors – and that that, briefly, is what the 'aggressive drive' is for. But those who were taken in by *On Aggression* might have had second thoughts had they known large chunks of it closely resemble a paper, written in 1942, with the Final Solution in full swing, when he was Professor of Psychology at the University of Königsberg in East Prussia.

'The Innate Forms of Possible Experience',[1] which has been omitted from the two volumes of his collected papers published in English, evoked *Gestalt* perception and the principles of ethology to recommend a 'self-conscious scientifically based race policy' to eliminate the degenerates who preyed on the healthy body of society like the profiteering growth of a malignant cancer. The arbiters of this scheme were to be 'our best individuals' (*Führer-Individuen*) whose intolerant value judgements would decide who was – or was not – stricken with decay. Lorenz rejected Spengler's pessimistic conclusion that nations declined through a logic inherent in time. Applied biology would forestall Spengler's 'inevitable fate'.

Then, as now, the greylag goose is pressed into the argument. A pure-blooded gander has 'a more sharply contoured head, straighter posture, redder feet, broader shoulders', etc., whereas a barnyard goose develops a stunted appearance, not to mention a complete breakdown of morals. Similiarly, he says, we admire in men tight hips, wide shoulders and an eagle-like stare.[2] And we recoil from the features of decay: 'Loss of muscle, shortening of the extremities, growth of fat and a quantitative increase of eating and copulation drives.' 'Not one feature of domestication do we *instinctively* approve of.'

Again, he illustrated the text with photographs; a fish from the stream, a wild greylag gander, a wolf and a bust portrait of Pericles – all long-featured – are juxtaposed against a pop-eyed goldfish, a domesticated goose, an Old English Bulldog (the date is 1942) and

---

[1] 'Die angeborenen Formen möglicher Erfahrung' in *Zeitschrift für Tierpsychologie*, Bd 5, Heft 2, 1943, p. 235 ff. In this work Lorenz's old father is quoted in a less genial mood: 'From the stand-point of racial biology, the whole of medical practice is a disaster for mankind.'

[2] This 'ideal form for our race' is illustrated with a photo of Arno Breker's epicene statue of Dionysus, a favourite of Hitler and Speer; the fact that savages had quite different canons of beauty merely proved their innate inability to acquire civilisation.

a marble head of Socrates – all of which had the squashed-up features of genetic decay.

The lesson of this paper was that it was positively heroic to act with intolerance: attempts to discover why you rejected a person simply obscured your original judgement. And he exhorted the racial biologists to be quick: 'There is indeed need to hurry!' – though there were more than two years left.

I quote this passage if only for the style:

Just as in the case of a surgeon who, in removing a growing cancer tumour, draws with his knife an arbitrary and 'unfair' sharp line between what is to be removed and what is to be preserved, and consciously prefers to remove healthy tissue than let diseased tissue remain, so must the *a priori* value judgement, when it comes to determine a frontier, decide on a point where plus is transformed into minus ...

There is a lot more to the paper, including a fantastic rigmarole that attempted to resolve the headache of every racial biologist. Why should the gene for beauty go sauntering off in a different direction from the gene for goodness? How was it that a perfect Teuton soul had nested in the body of the Führer? – to say nothing of the fact that by 1942 the racists had to accommodate the Japanese?

Of course, one could dismiss all this as a temporary, if lethally ingenious, aberration, had Lorenz not continued to churn out many of the same ideas, the same metaphors, sometimes even the same passages – doctored here and there for postwar sensibilities – from 1950 to the present day. For example, when he discusses the 'social fighting reaction' in *On Aggression*, he regrets the misuse of this primaeval drive by demagogues and hopes that 'our moral responsibility may gain control over it'. In a paper written in

1950[1] he says that anyone is pleased to find a substitute, or 'dummy', as a target for his pent-up aggression, adding that 'without this purely physiological basis all of the past cases of demagogically directed mass cruelty, such as witchcraft trials or anti-Semitic persecution', would not have been possible. But in 1942 he had only an exhortation to offer: 'I accuse any young man who has not experienced this reaction on politically significant occasions of emotional weakness!'

In 1942 he never named the Jews. He could, arguably, have been referring to the Euthanasia Programme which did away with about 70,000 Gentile degenerates before the Nazis set to work elsewhere. But then Lorenz usually appeals to general principle, not to the sordid detail of a particular problem.

Going through Daniel Gasman's brilliant and disturbing book *The Scientific Origins of National Socialism*, one is struck, also, by how few of Lorenz's ideas on human behaviour rest on 'inductive natural science' but how many of them repeat the tenets of Monism,[2] the movement created by the biologist Ernst Haeckel to interpret Darwinism for social purposes and to combat socialist ideologies as contrary to nature's plan. The Monists were the first to attempt a fusion of biology and social science, and it was under the umbrella of Monist ideas that German academic circles were united with the most strident demands of German nationalism. The point made by Gasman, which cannot be emphasised too strongly, is that the Nazis believed in the final solution as 'scientific' and thus sanctioned by Natural Law.[3]

Alfred North Whitehead once wrote: 'Nature is patient of interpretation in terms of laws that happen to interest us.' And

[1] 'Part and Parcel in Animal and Human Societies', in Lorenz, *Studies in Animal and Human Behaviour* (Harvard University Press, 1971), Vol. II, pp. 115–95.

[2] 'Monism', as opposed to 'Dualism', signifying the indivisibility of man from the rest of nature – often very similar, in form and content, to the new sociobiology.

[3] *The Scientific Origins of National Socialism: Social Darwinism in Ernst Haeckel and the German Monist League* (MacDonald, London; N. Watson, N.Y., 1971).

Lorenz's career is surely a warning to anyone who presumes to write an objective 'biogrammer' or 'ethological paradigm' for the human species. For it shows just how far the 'facts' of our evolutionary past can be stretched or patterned to conform with the wilder flights of prejudice.

In a historical context, Lorenzian ethology falls into the category of what Lovejoy and Boas called 'Animalitarianism' – 'the tendency to represent the beasts – on one ground or another – as creatures more admirable, more normal, or more fortunate than the human species.'[1] That man himself is a flawed, aberrant being, that his Fall occurred even before he became human, is a constant theme in Western thought from the fourth century BC onward, especially among societies which have lost their nerve. For if the concept of the Good Savage encouraged reformers of a levelling temper to hope for a simpler and more equable life, the Myth of the Happier Beast damned hopes for a better world, engendered in man a disgust for himself and his works, absolved him from responsibility for his actions, and led him, in his desperate search for remedies, to fall into a collective moral anaesthesia and bow his neck to tyranny.

1979

---

[1] Arthur O. Lovejoy and George Boas, *Primitivism and Related Ideas in Antiquity* (rcpr. Octagon Books, 1965), pp. 19–22.

V

ART AND THE
IMAGE-BREAKER

AMONG THE RUINS

On the island of Capri there lived three narcissists who each built a house on the edge of a cliff. They were Axel Munthe, Baron Jacques Adelswärd-Fersen and Curzio Malaparte. All three were writers of the self-dramatising variety. All had a strong dose of Nordic sensibility. And all sought to expand their personalities in architecture. Their houses were thus acts of self-love – 'dream houses' where they hoped to live, love, and work wonders of creation, but which, despite idyllic settings, were infected by a morbid atmosphere akin to that of Böcklin's *Island of the Dead*.

Capri is, of course, the 'Isle of Goats'. At the time of the Emperor Tiberius it was still a Greek enclave, and the illusion persisted into modern times that the Great (goat-footed) God Pan was not entirely dead, that Capri was still a pagan paradise in a Catholic sea, where the wine was excellent, the sun always shone, and the boys and girls were pretty and available. From the mid-nineteenth century on, a rush of romantically minded northerners descended on Capri – to buy, build or rent a villa.

There were German artists, English middle-class eccentrics, American lesbians and Russian 'god builders'. Kaiser Wilhelm II came; so, at one time or another, did D. H. Lawrence, Rilke, Field Marshal Rommel, Edda Ciano, Gracie Fields and Lord Alfred Douglas (who sat it out in a villa while Oscar Wilde was in Reading Gaol).

Or there was Norman Douglas – scholar, hedonist, and

absolutely no relation of Alfred's – who, having lost his own villa in a financial tumble, preferred the convenience of rented rooms. Or Fritz Krupp, the 'Cannon King', who built himself a cliffside garçonnière – only to commit suicide when his homosexuality was noised about by a Naples newspaper. Or Maxim Gorky, who wrote *Mother* on Capri. Or Gorky's good friend Lenin, a popular fisherman known locally as Signor Drindrin.

But the key to Capri's history is the Emperor Tiberius. He owned twelve villas on the island, some in the hills, others by the sea. At his cliff-top palace, Villa Jovis, he built a lighthouse from which he could flash commands relayed to all quarters of the empire.

Tiberius' character is an academic battleground. Was he – as Norman Douglas believed – the shy, frugal, scholarly, mob-hating and art-loving ascetic who startled his Greek philosopher friends by asking what songs the Sirens usually sang, and who found he could cope with government only by retiring to his airy pavilions, to be alone with his thoughts and his books? Or was he – as described by Suetonius – the hideous old pederast, whose left hand was so strong he 'could poke a finger through a sound, freshly plucked apple, or into the skull of a boy or young man'?

Did he collect sexual athletes from all over the empire? Did he swim in grottoes with corrupted children? Did he play games with his victims before having them chucked from the Salto di Tiberio, a thousand feet into the sea?

Given the tenuous borderline between extremes of asceticism and of sensuality, the 'good' Tiberius is probably the same as the 'bad'. But it was the second, Suetonian Tiberius who inspired the Marquis de Sade, an early tourist on the island, to write a couple of sizzling debauches for the characters Justine and Juliette, and who also provoked Baron Jacques Adelswärd-Fersen, a young aesthete awash with dreams of future orgies, to build his Villa Lysis (or La Gloriette) on a tongue of land below the emperor's Villa Jovis.

'It is one of my many crimes,' wrote Norman Douglas in *Looking Back*, 'that I induced this apple of discord to establish himself on Capri. No: that is putting it too strongly. The fact is he turned up on the island one day and met me almost immediately. He was about twenty-three years old.'

Fersen's life has been dealt with in two novels, Compton Mackenzie's *Vestal Fire* and Roger Peyrefitte's *L'Exilé de Capri* – the result of which has been that the 'real' Fersen has vanished into a lilac mist. *Vestal Fire* is a straightforward *roman à clef* (it must have seemed quite risky when it came out) which charts the incestuous comings and goings of an expatriate island colony treated to the irruption of an absurd French count, Robert Marsac, and his Italian boyfriend, Carlo. Peyrefitte's book, on the other hand, confuses famous historical figures with imaginary situations and is maddening to read.

Fersen apparently belonged to the same family as 'le beau Fersen', the Swedish aristocrat and presumed lover of Marie-Antoinette whose attempt to rescue the royal family ended in the fiasco at Varennes. A cadet branch of the Fersens settled in the France of Napoleon III and founded a steel mill near Luxembourg. Jacques's father died at sea. Jacques was the only son, and was thus a very rich young man.

He grew up in Paris of the 1890s and seems to have modelled himself on Robert de Montesquiou (who also was the model for Des Esseintes and Baron de Charlus). He had, according to Norman Douglas, a 'childish freshness' and blue eyes, and was always overtailored. His first volume of verse was circulated in respectable homes, despite its morbid tone and the poet's penchant for pink roses, or pink in general ('Et nous serons des morts sous des vêtements roses'), an affectation derived, at a guess, from Montesquiou's *Les Hortensias Bleus*.

His troubles began with the publication of *Hymnaire d'Adonis – Paganismes – à la Façon de M. le Marquis de Sade*. He was, however, about to forswear these frivolities and marry a Mlle de Maupeou when, without warning, the police arrested him for the corruption of schoolboys in his apartment on the Avenue de Friedland.

This episode is the subject of Fersen's own semi-autobiographical farrago of 1905, *Lord Lyllian, ou Messes Noires*, which Norman Douglas describes as having a 'musty, Dorian-Grayish flavour' and which is not without unconscious humour.

Tried, sentenced, and then released, Fersen fled to Italy, where he met two American ladies, the Wolcott-Perry 'sisters', who invited him to their villa on Capri. He then decided, as an act of defiance, to build his own dream house; and when Norman Douglas showed him the site under Monte Tiberio, Fersen said, 'One could write poetry here.' He refused to be deterred even when warned that the house would get no more than two hours of sunshine a day in winter. While the building went up he travelled to Ceylon, where he picked up an opium habit. Then he picked up a newspaper boy in Rome, whom he installed on Capri as his secretary.

The boy's name was Nino Cesarini, and he had to put up with a lot. Fersen had 'some loveable streaks', according to Douglas: he was not 'disingenuous or false, but theatrical'. He was also vain, empty-headed and stingy. He mounted exotic festivities and quarrelled with all his guests. He forbade Nino to flirt with girls yet persisted in parading him round the island as if he were an ancient bronze Apollo. He took him to China, where they bought a collection of some three hundred opium pipes. He took him to Sicily to be photographed by Baron von Gloeden. Finally – if the story is true – he staged a mock human sacrifice in the Mithraic grotto of Matromania, with Nino as victim, and both of them were booted off the island.

When war broke out in 1914, Nino had to be detoxified from opium and went off to fight in the Apennines, while Fersen stayed in the south of France. Eventually he was allowed back to the Villa Lysis; but he had quarrelled with the Wolcott-Perrys, who shut their doors on him, and in addition to opium, he took to cocaine.

After the war Nino came back to care for his master, who, despite an illusion of perennial youth, was by this time very ill. 'This house of mine', Fersen said, 'has the flavour of death.' One stormy night in November 1923, 'Count Jack' (as Fersen was known on the island), dressed in robes of rose-coloured silk, lolled back on the cushions of his subterranean opium den. Nino, who had gone to the kitchen, returned to find him semi-conscious. 'How many grams?' he shouted. 'How many grams?' 'Five,' murmured Fersen, unclenching his fist as he slipped away – at least that was the version printed in the Naples daily *Il Mattino*.

Fersen's family stripped the villa, used it for the odd picnic, and then sold it to a Levantine businessman. 'There it stands,' wrote Norman Douglas in 1933, 'like a castle in a tale, all empty and forlorn, and embowered or rather smothered in a tangle of trees … because he grew so fond of his pines and ilexes and mimosas that he would not allow the smallest twig of them to be touched.'

And there it stands, or half-stands, in its dark, 'holy' wood, again for sale – this alien 'French' folly, which a Capriote wit once called the 'visiting card of a courtesan', with its cracked stucco and splintering jalousies, silent but for the miaowing of cats, the crowing of cockerels, and the drone of powerboats in the sea below.

I found altars in the overgrown garden, and a *temple de l'amour*. (A relic of impossible yearnings? Of Versailles and the queen?) The concrete urns had come adrift of their rusty armatures and lay in little pieces in the grass. And in the colonnade under the salon, the villa's guardian had laid out carob pods to dry, and had tied up her sad beige dog.

She was a lithe young woman, jealous of her estate. She had a green thumb. In olive-oil cans she grew geraniums, pelargoniums, and canna lilies, which flowered with an almost supernatural brilliance on the steps below the portico. The house was in shadow. A black cat kept crossing my path, as if to warn me not to trespass. There were cats everywhere, puffy-faced cats, and the smell of cat piss. And there were banks of blue hydrangeas – *les hortensias bleus* of Montesquiou.

I found the salon's colour scheme had been white and blue and gold. But the roof had caved in and heaps of rubble now covered the chambre chinoise, with its yellow tiles and phony Chinese inscriptions, where Fersen once arranged his pipes in lacquered racks.

Yet outside, the gold mosaic still clung to the fluted columns, and, over the peristyle, I could still read, in black marble letters, AMORI ET DOLORI SACRUM – 'Sacred to Love and Sorrow'. And the white marble stair, balustraded with vine leaves and purple grapes, still led to Nino's nusery-like bedroom – although Jacques's had tumbled down.

He was said to be the 'most fascinating man in Europe', but it is hard, in retrospect, to like Axel Munthe or his pretentious museum-sanctuary, the Villa San Michele.

Born in 1857 in the Swedish province of Småland, Munthe came from a family of bishops and burgomasters which had moved to Scandinavia from Flanders. He studied medicine at Uppsala University and, at the age of eighteen, travelled to Italy to recover from a haemorrhaging lung. Happening to spend a day in the town of Anacapri, he saw an abandoned chapel and beside it a garden whose owner, Mastro Vincenzo, had unearthed the mosaic floors of a Roman villa and a lot of ancient marble fragments – the *roba di Timberio*, or 'things of Tiberius', as they were called by local peasants. Munthe recognised the site as one of

Tiberius' twelve and conceived, there and then if one believes him, a mission to own it.

'Why should I not buy Mastro Vincenzo's house,' he wrote in *The Story of San Michele*, 'and join the chapel and the house with garlands of vines and avenues of cypresses and columns supporting white loggias, peopled with marble statues of gods and bronzes of emperors.'

Munthe did not go back to Sweden but continued his studies in Montpellier and then in Paris. At twenty-two he was the youngest doctor of medicine in France. He had charm, intelligence and a most plausible bedside manner, and he was soon the partner in a fashionable practice. He believed in making the rich pay for the poor. He took a special interest in nervous diseases and their possible cure by hypnosis.

He was the close friend of Prince Eugen Bernardotte, the Swedish king's youngest son, who was then leading the life of artistic bohemia in Paris. He knew Strindberg. He knew Maupassant (and even cruised on his yacht): in fact, much of *The Story of San Michele* – with its high life, low life, and whiffs of the supernatural – reminds one of Maupassant's late style. In 1884 Munthe interrupted a journey through Lapland to work in the poor districts of Naples during a cholera epidemic. In 1889 he left Paris, bought the land at San Michele, and, to pay for the villa, set up another practice, in Keats' house, off the Piazza di Spagna in Rome.

There he prospered. Dr Weir Mitchell sent him ailing millionairesses from the United States. From Vienna, Professor Krafft-Ebing sent him neuropaths 'of both sexes and of no sex'. His fees were colossal, his celebrated 'cures' perhaps due less to conventional medicine than to changes of climate and scenery. He collected royalty as he collected antiquities. His principal patient was Queen Victoria of Sweden, whom he cajoled into living far longer than she apparently intended. The Czarina craved his attentions, for herself and the haemophiliac Czarevitch (to the extent of almost kidnapping Munthe aboard the imperial yacht), and when he refused her, she fell into the arms of Rasputin.

There were times when the villa on Capri must have seemed like a sanatorium for ailing queens and empresses; the Empress Elisabeth of Austria was dying to buy it. Later, when the supply of royalty began to dry up, their successors continued to call.

'As for San Michele itself,' Munthe wrote, ironically and in English, to Hermann Goering in August 1937, 'I should be glad to lend it to you if ever you can get away from your tremendous cares. The place is small. It was built by me on the principle that the soul needs more room than the body, and it may not be comfortable enough for you.'

He was his own architect: the style he chose was Saracen-Romanesque. The house was white and light – a 'sanctuary to the sun' – and done up in the 'Renaissance' manner most popular around the turn of the century. (Roberto Pane, the architectural historian of Capri, has described it as '*un falso presuntuoso quanto insultante*'.) There was indeed a loggia peopled with statues – genuine and fake – of gods and emperors, and fragments of ancient marble, some salvaged from the imperial villa, were stuck into the walls like nuts in nougat.

He laid out gardens with pergolas, terraces and cypress walks. And as to the Chapel of San Michele itself, which used to stand like a lonely, cliff-top hermitage, he had it transformed into a kind of pasha's pavilion from which he could gaze up to the Castle of Barbarossa, down over the cliffs to Marina Grande, or across the bay to Tiberius' Villa Jovis – and that execrated blot on the landscape, Fersen's Villa Lysis.

At San Michele the view is everything: in Pasadena or Beverly Hills Munthe's creation wouldn't get more than a passing glance. Yet it is still one of the best-loved houses in the world, and after fifty-five years *The Story of San Michele* is still a best-seller and has been translated into some fifty languages (its Korean translator had turned up shortly before my visit).

Munthe was a natural storyteller who, before hypnotising others, had taken great pains to hypnotise himself. He spun tales of buried treasure; of madness; of mixed-up coffins; of wordly clerics, cold countesses and good-hearted whores; of the nun he nearly seduced during the cholera epidemic. What, however, made the book irresistible, particularly to its English readers, was Munthe's passionate identification with birds and animals. He rescued a baboon from its half-crazed American owner. He almost killed in a duel a sadistic French viscount who had kicked Munthe's dog so severely the animal had to be shot. He declared war on the butcher of Anacapri, who would net migrant birds and blind them with red-hot needles to make them sing. And finally, he succeeded in persuading Mussolini to turn the whole of Capri into a bird sanctuary.

From a literary point of view, the book's best stories deal with his years in Paris and Rome and are told with a clinical, world-weary detachment; they are reminiscent of (besides Maupassant) another doctor turned writer, W. Somerset Maugham. Like Maugham, too, his reminiscences always seem to wind up on a self-congratulatory (or, later, self-pitying) note; and the book in general bears out Oscar Wilde's warning of the pitfalls of the first-person narrative, particularly when the narrator is a compulsive mythomaniac.

Munthe was besotted by Tiberius. According to Levente Erdeös, the director of the San Michele Foundation on Capri, 'He had a kind of disease, to me, more or less obsessed by the late emperor. He could look down from his loggia and think that he, also, was the ruler of the world.' Tiberius had owned twelve houses on the island; Munthe had to have twelve. Tiberius was a collector of statues; Munthe had to have statues too. But instead of admitting these came from ordinary antique dealers in Naples and elsewhere, he preferred to veil his 'discoveries' in mystery.

He liked to insinuate that the bronze copy of the Lysippan Hermes (which sits at the end of the loggia and was given to him by the city of Naples for his help with the cholera) was not, in fact, a copy but the original, which had been deliberately spirited out of the museum by one of his adoring well-wishers.

Another time he 'felt' that a face was watching him from the sea-bed; and when he trained his telescope on a pale speck offshore, it turned out to be the marble Medusa head now set into the wall behind his desk. Or there was the huge basalt Horus falcon – 'the largest I have ever seen,' he wrote, 'brought from the land of the Pharaohs by some Roman collector, maybe by Tiberius himself'. Yet this object, so far as I could judge, was a standard fake from the Cairo bazaar.

By the 1920s Munthe had become a British subject. He had worked with the British Red Cross in Flanders during the First World War. And in 1943, fearing perhaps that the Germans would invade Italy, he left for Stockholm (on the same plane as Curzio Malaparte, who was travelling as a journalist to the Finno-Soviet front). He did not come back. His friend King Gustav V gave him a suite of rooms in the royal palace; and there, dreaming of the South, he died, on 11 February 1949. He had been anxious that San Michele should remain a monument to himself, and bequeathed it to the Swedish state. A memorial plaque reads: 'To the Everlasting Memory of Dr Axel Munthe. His life – A radiant symbol of perfect humanity.' The place is thronged with tourists, and kept as clean as a clinic.

Nowadays not many islanders remember the old doctor, who would stroll around town in the shabby clothes that marked him out as a *signore*. I did, however, pick up the following:

From a *grande dame*: 'He was insatiable. We used to call him *Il*

Caprone – "The Billy Goat"! And not just for that! He smelled something terrible.'

From a Neapolitan prince: 'It was a bad crossing. How would you say that in English? A bad mixture! He populated half of Anacapri, and they all had red hair and horse faces. Sometimes you'd hear the children shouting, "Horse face!" "Horse face!" – and you knew they were shouting at one of Munthe's bastards.'

From the omniscient young historian who works in the town hall of Anacapri: '*Era bisessuale*.'

The pro-Munthe faction, on the other hand, reveres his memory in hushed tones and piously enumerates his benefactions. In Anacapri I met one of these self-confessed 'Munthesians', who dashed about the garden of San Michele, pointing out this or that 'typically Munthesian detail' and the graves of the Queen of Sweden's dogs. He was quite upset that I had made a few inquiries elsewhere.

'They know nothing,' he said crossly. 'They are jealous of Munthe. They are jealous of the man and his achievements. You must ask me. I know everything.'

'Was he a cold fish?' I asked.

'A fish?'

'A cold person?'

'He was hot and cold. He was all things.'

'In what way does he interest you?'

'He was interesting.'

'But how?'

'He was a pioneer of ecology. He went to Mussolini to stop the people killing birds.'

'What else?'

'He was the creator of beauty.'

'Where?'

'He created this spot.'

Curzio Malaparte was a very strange writer, and his villa, which he built in the years 1938–40 on the lonely headland of Capo Massullo, is one of the strangest habitations in the Western world.

A 'Homeric' ship gone aground? A modern altar to Poseidon? A house of the future – or of the prehistoric past? A surrealist house? A Fascist house? Or a 'Tiberian' refuge from a world gone mad? Is it the house of the dandy and professional joker, the *Arcitaliano*, as he was known to his friends – or of the melancholy German romantic who lay masked underneath? The 'pure' house of an ascetic? Or the anxious private theatre of an insatiable Casanova? What we do know is that Malaparte asked his architect, Adalberto Libera, to build him a '*casa come me*' – a 'house like me' – which would be '*triste, dura, severa*', as 'sad, hard and severe' as he hoped himself to be. He had his notepaper headed, in thick black letters, CASA COME ME – and indeed, down to the last petit bourgeois detail, the house is a biography of its owner.

Curzio Malaparte, born in 1898, was baptised Kurt Suckert. His father, Erwin Suckert, was an irritable small-time textile manufac-turer from Saxony who had settled in Prato, near Florence, and married a Florentine woman.

Early photos of Kurt show a sleek, beautiful, black-haired young man confronting the camera with the ironic and disdainful demeanour of certain portraits by Bronzino. By 1913 he was already frequenting the Red Coats café in Florence, where intellectual hotheads clamoured for action, any kind of action, in a Europe so satiated with peace that it had come to think that peace was immoral. When war broke out, he enlisted in the Legione Garibaldina and distinguished himself under fire: like Hemingway (who was a year his junior), on the Austrian front; then at Bligny, near Rheims, where nearly ten thousand Italians were killed and he himself got a gas-damaged lung.

After the war he became a journalist and a Fascist. He joined the march on Rome and signed the first Manifesto of Fascist

Intellectuals. Antonio Gramsci, co-founder of the Italian Communist Party, knew him at this time and delivered a harsh verdict on his frantic *arrivismo*, immeasurable vanity, and chameleon-like snobbery: 'To have success [he] would do any kind of mischief.' In 1925 Suckert read a nineteenth-century pamphlet titled, in part, *I Malaparte e i Bonaparte* and changed his name.

Malaparte fancied himself a 'man of action' rather in the mould of T.E. Lawrence or André Malraux. He shared their flair for self-advertisement and their mythomania; yet when it came to the crunch, the role he chose was not that of participant but that of literary voyeur. He was astute enough to see, from the start, the cruel absurdities of Mussolini's movement; and with his corrosive sense of humour he could never resist the temptation to mock men in power. The first hint of trouble came when he mocked Mussolini's taste in ties. The Duce called him to his office in the Palazzo Chigi to apologise. Then, crossing the cold marble floor after the interview, Malaparte turned and said:

'Permit me to say one last word in my defence.'

'Go ahead,' said Mussolini, raising his eyes.'

'Even today you're wearing a horrible tie.'

Malaparte loved princesses and peasants; he hated homosexuals and his own humdrum background. He was a sharp dresser. (With one of his old friends, the Principe di Sirignano, I had a discussion as to whether he used to anoint his hair with brilliantine or Vaseline or *la gomina argentina*.) He could mesmerise any room with his stories; and the highly placed Fascists who were his protectors were secretly delighted to hear the Duce jeered at. In 1929 Senator Giovanni Agnelli, the chairman of Fiat and no friend of the régime, appointed him editor-in-chief of Agnelli's newspaper, *La Stampa*.

For two years, until his forcible dismissal, Malaparte used it as a sniping post.

He had developed a theory that the wars and revolutions of the

twentieth century, far from being the products of the contra-
dictions inherent in bourgeois capitalism, were compounded
from the disgust and envy of the bourgeoisie for itself. The
Russian Revolution was a European phenomenon. Lenin was
not some new Asiatic Chingis Khan but 'a timid and fanatical'
bourgeois functionary, a small man, part German like himself.

He carried his thesis to its conclusion in a small, brilliant book,
the *Technique du Coup d'État*, which he published in Paris in 1931,
after the Fascists forced him to leave *La Stampa*. The final chapter,
written two years before the Nazis took power in Germany,
carried the arresting title 'Une Femme: Hitler':

> That fat and boastful Austrian … with hard mistrustful eyes,
> fixed ambitions and cynical plans, could well have, like all
> Austrians, a certain taste for the heroes of Ancient Rome …
>
> His hero, Julius Caesar in *Lederhosen* …
>
> Hitler is a caricature of Mussolini …
>
> The spirit of Hitler is profoundly feminine; his intelligence,
> his ambitions, even his willpower have nothing virile about
> them …
>
> Dictatorship … is the most complete form of envy in all its
> aspects, political, moral, intellectual …
>
> Hitler, the dictator; the woman whom Germany deserves …

None of this endeared him to the Duce, and, in Malaparte's
own words, 'Hitler asked for my head and got it.' On returning,
courageously or misguidedly, from Paris in 1933, he was accused
of anti-Fascist activities abroad, arrested, beaten up, put in the
Regina Coeli jail, and, like some disgraced senator of imperial
Rome, sentenced to five years' exile on the island of Lipari.

Here, guarded by *carabinièri*, he read Homer and Plato in the
original, while the waves crashed onto the grey volcanic beach
outside his house. Pictures show him in immaculate white plus

fours but no socks, puckering his face like a middle-aged matador and caressing his favourite terrier:

> I had no one but the dogs to talk to. At night I went out onto the terrace of my sad house by the sea. I leaned over the balustrade and called out Eolo, the brother of my own dog Febo. I called Vulcano, and Apollo, and Stromboli ... All the dogs had ancient names ... the dogs of my fishermen friends. I stayed for hours on my terrace, howling at the dogs who howled back at me ...

Malaparte makes a lot of capital out of the five-year sentence: 'Too much sea, too much sky, for so small an island and so restless a spirit.' The truth was that after about a year his friend Galeazzo Ciano, Mussolini's son-in-law, managed to have him transferred to Ischia and then to Forte del Marmi, where he lived in a villa with Febo, entertained, had the use of a ministerial Alfa-Romeo, and wrote satirical articles under the pseudonym Candido. For all Mussolini's faults, he was not vindictive, or without a sense of the absurd. Secretly he seems to have liked Malaparte – but was obliged to defer to the Germans.

Once the 'exile' was over, Malaparte bought his own house in Forte dei Marmi, the Villa Hildebrand, which had been built for a German sculptor and frescoed by Böcklin. He then founded *Prospettive*, a cultural review with a bias toward surrealism, and published Pound, André Breton, Alberto Moravia, Mario Praz, De Chirico and Paul Éluard.

He went to Africa as a war correspondent during the Ethiopian campaign. On the whole, his dispatches were not unfavourable to Mussolini. He had also written a collection of autobiographical fantasies with such titles as 'A Woman Like Me', 'A Dog Like Me', 'A Land Like Me', 'A Saint Like Me'. And in a somewhat mysterious manner he had laid his hands on a sizeable sum of money. He bought Capo Massullo from a Capriote fisherman, saying that he wanted to keep rabbits there; instead he commissioned Libera to build the 'house like me'.

Casa Come Me, with its stupendous views of sea and sky and rock, was intended to satisfy his 'melancholic yearning for space' and at the same time to reproduce, on his own grandiose terms, the conditions of his exile on Lipari. It was to be the monastery-bunker of the man who had faced the dictators alone – a *casamatta*, a 'blockhouse' or 'madhouse', depending on which way you read that word in Italian; a house of the machine age that would nevertheless preserve the most ancient values of the Mediterranean. And unlike the 'Apollonian' temples of classical Greece, with their forests of columns and 'roofs set down from above', this building was to rise, like a Minoan sanctuary, from the sea itself.

The walls were the colour of bull's blood, the windows were like the windows of a liner, and there was a wedge-shaped ramp of steps which slanted, like a sacred way, up to the terrace roof. Here, every morning, Malaparte would perform a ritual of gymnastics, alone, while the women who were in love with him would watch from the cliffs above.

Inside the house, on the upper floor, was the vast whitewashed atrium-saloon, its stone floors strewn with chamois skins, its long suede sofas with loose linen covers, and its wave-edged 'Minoan' tables resting on concrete columns. There were huge, wooden, 'fascistic' sculptures of nudes by Pericle Fazzini; and through the plate-glass fireback of the fireplace his guests could watch the sea behind the flames.

Beyond were the writer's own quarters and the 'Room of the Favourite', each with its bathroom of veined grey marble fit for the murder of Agamemnon. Malaparte seems to have treated sex as something solemn and sacramental; in the Room of the Favourite the double bed is stationed against a plain, panelled wall and looks like the altar of a Cistercian monastery. The study too, despite its faience stove, its painting of Ethiopian women, and its floor tiles painted with the lyre of Orpheus, has a liturgical flavour. It was in this room, in September 1943, that Malaparte finished *Kaputt*, '[my] horribly gay and gruesome book', which made his reputation outside Italy.

On Mussolini's declaration of war, Ciano advised his friend to get into uniform. So, as captain of the Fifth Alpine Regiment, Malaparte went first to watch the Italian invasion of Greece, then to report for the *Corriere della Sera* on the Russian front. He managed to charm or flatter his way into high Nazi circles. At Cracow, on the Vistula, he dined with Reichsminister Frank, the butcher of Poland, who assured him that he, Frank, was to be Poland's Orpheus, who would 'win these people over by the arts, poetry and music'. Malaparte also wormed his way into the Warsaw ghetto and reported, somewhat evasively, what he had seen. He followed the Panzer divisions into the Ukraine and witnessed the senseless atrocities there.

His articles, syndicated through Sweden to the rest of the world, hinted from the outset that Germany was doomed. The Gestapo pressed for his removal, or worse; but Mussolini, already squirming under the shadow of Hitler, allowed him instead to go to Finland to report on the Finno-Soviet war. In the summer of 1943, on hearing of the Duce's fall, Malaparte flew from Stockholm to Italy. By the time the Americans arrived in Naples, he was sitting calmly in Casa Come Me, writing.

In *Kaputt* Malaparte chose to present an aesthete's view of German-occupied Europe, describing it as some vast and sinister fresco of the dance of death. The result, to say the least, is disturbing. His angle of vision is always oblique, always equivocal; the tone is surrealist – or, like the Nazis themselves, kitsch. There are moments when the imagery of Dali seems, at last, to have found a real-life subject, such as a scene in which Malaparte shared a sauna with Himmler, or this visit to the *Poglavnik* (military governor) of Croatia, after a push by the partisans:

'The Croatian people,' said Ante Pavelič, 'wish to be ruled with goodness and justice. And I am here to provide them.'

While he spoke, I gazed at a wicker basket on the Poglavnik's desk. The lid was raised and the basket seemed to be filled with mussels, or shelled oysters – as they are occasionally displayed in the windows of Fortnum and Mason in Piccadilly in London. Casertano, an Italian diplomat, looked at me and winked, 'Would you like a nice oyster stew?'

'Are they Dalmatian oysters?' I asked the Poglavnik.

Ante Pavelič removed the lid from the basket and revealed the mussels, that slimy jelly-like mass, and he said smiling, with that tired good-natured smile of his, 'It is a present from my loyal *ustashis*. Forty pounds of human eyes.'

Now, to my mind, the combination of 'forty pounds' and 'Fortnum and Mason' is both nauseating and bogus; and however weird *Kaputt* may seem on first reading, it surely works neither as novel nor as memoir. The same goes for *Kaputt*'s sequel, *The Skin*, a book written in a similarly self-inflationary vein, and one which tells of his career as a liaison officer between the Italian army and its new-found American allies. The set pieces, this time around, are sadistic 'southern baroque'.

The Skin was an international best-seller – except among the Neapolitans and Capriotes, who, feeling themselves to have been calumniated by a collaborator, made Malaparte's life on the island extremely uncomfortable. He joined the Communist Party, became disillusioned, and decided to emigrate to France.

There he fared no better. He loathed the intellectual climate of Paris during the reign of Camus and Sartre. He wrote a play about Proust, and another about Karl Marx in London; both were booed off the stage. He returned to Italy to make a successful film. People remember him at literary gatherings in Rome, in a well-cut brown tweed jacket, with a silent, boyish girl on his arm. He started to get fat and planned to ride a bicycle from New York to Los Angeles. Finally, in 1956, he went to the Soviet Union and China, where he wrote sober reportage, suggesting that he could have become a new kind of writer, not necessarily at the centre of things.

On Sunday, the eleventh of November, he fell ill with fever in Peking. The doctor who attended him said, 'You have caught a gentle little Chinese microbe which has given you … a gentle little Chinese fever. Nothing serious.' It was an incurable cancer of the lung. On his deathbed he converted to Catholicism and received the final absolution.

'How he prayed!' said the Principe di Sirignano. 'He prayed to Christ … to the Madonna of Pompeii … to Lenin … But he died in agony!'

He left Casa Come Me – perhaps out of malice towards the Capriotes – for the use of artists from the People's Republic of China. His family contested the will, got the house back, and has recently set up a Malaparte foundation, whose function was not exactly clear to me. On the day of my visit the house was full of art students from Munich.

I also met a local man who said that Malaparte had been a big boss of the Communist Party.

'Can't you see it?' he said, looking down the cliff at the rectangular roof and its curving concrete windbreak. 'He built the house in the shape of a hammer and sickle.'

1984

THE MORALITY OF THINGS

This morning we have assembled to bow before the graven image. But an Old Testament prophet, were he present, would have thundered, 'Fingers Off! Thou shalt not lust after things.' The patriarchs of Ancient Israel lived in black tents. Their wealth was in herds; they moved up and down their tribal lands on seasonal migrations; and they were famous for their resistance to art objects. They would have stormed into art galleries as they stormed into the shrines of Baal, and slashed every image in sight. And this, not because they couldn't pack them in their saddle-bags, but on moral grounds. For they believed that pictures separated man from God. The adoration of images was a sin of settlement; the worship of the Golden Calf had satisfied the emotional weaklings who sighed for the fleshpots of Egypt. And prophets like Isaiah and Jeremiah recalled the time when their people were a race of hardy individualists, who did not need to comfort themselves with images. For this reason they denounced the Temple which God's Children had turned into a sculpture gallery, and recommended a policy of vandalism and a return to the tents.

And do we not all long to throw down our altars and rid ourselves of our possessions? Do we not gaze coldly at our clutter and say, 'If these objects express my personality, then I hate my personality.' For what, on the face of it, enhances life less than a work of art? One tires of it. One cannot eat it. It makes an uncomfortable bedfellow. One guards it, and feels obliged to enjoy it long after it has ceased to amuse. We sacrifice our freedom of action to become its privileged guardian, and we end its imprisoned slave. All civilisations are by their very nature 'thing-oriented' and the main problem of their stability has been to devise new equations between the urge to amass things and the urge to be rid of them.

But things have a way of insinuating themselves into all human lives. Some people attract more things than others, but no people, however mobile, is *thingless*. A chimpanzee uses sticks and stones as tools, but he does not keep possessions. Man does. And the things to which he becomes most attached do not serve any useful function. Instead they are symbols or emotional anchors. The question I should like to ask (without necessarily being able to answer it) is, 'Why are man's real treasures useless?' For if we understood this, we might also understand the convoluted rituals of the art market.

People who know and really love things – people, we say, who have taste – commonly rant against the philistine who buys a work of art with as much emotion as he would eat an egg. They accuse him of collecting in order to buy an intellectual respectability without having to suffer for it, or of making people admire him through the refracted mirror of his things. But Freud and the psychoanalysts have had far nastier innuendoes to make about the compulsive art collector. The true collector, they imply, is a voyeur in life, protected by a stuffing of possessions from those he would like to love, possessed of the tenderest emotions for things and glacial emotions for people. He is the classic cold fish. He taps the vitality of former ages to compensate for the impotence of the present. And he protects his things with defensive fury from the human wolves who threaten them. (We shall recall Karl Marx's insight that the destruction of brick and mortar causes more dismay to the bourgeois than the widespread spilling of human blood.) In other words, the collector evolves a moral system from which he squeezes out people. We can call it the morality of things.

The acquisition of an object in itself becomes a Grail Quest – the chase, the recognition of the quarry, the decision to purchase, the sacrifice and fear of financial ruin, the Dark Cloud of Unknowing ('Is it a fake?'), the wrapping, the journey home, the ecstasy of undressing the package, the object of the quest unveiled, the night one didn't go to bed with anyone, but kept vigil, gazing, stroking, adoring the new fetish – the companion, the lover, but very shortly *the bore*, to be kicked out or sold off while another more desirable thing supplants itself in our affections. I have often noticed that in the really great collections the best objects congregate like a host of guardian angels around the bed, and the bed itself is pitifully narrow. The true collector houses a corps of inanimate lovers to shore up the wreckage of life. In a self-analysis of surgical precision, Signor Mario Praz, in his *House of Life*, explains that people are never reliable. Instead one should surround oneself with things, for they never let you down.

The art collection, then, is a desperate stratagem against a failure, a personal ritual to cure loneliness. The art market is the public aspect of this private religion, and, with its apparent irrationality, seems to defy any known rule of commerce. It reduces businessmen into credulous believers, and makes the peasant with his pot of gold at the end of the rainbow seem positively hard-headed. Consider an important international art auction. Is it not some seasonal, liturgical drama? An uninitiated observer might imagine he was attending an arcane ceremony of mystic love. He would find an altar and a pulpit, the missals of service, the executant priest, his acolytes, the sacrament proffered, the slippery path along which many tread but few are chosen, the complex relationship between the priest-lover and his suitors, or between the seducer and seduced, the nervous anticipation, the esoteric numerology, the ascensionalism of the price, the crescendo, the moment of breathlessness, and (BANG) the climax!

We are told to the point of exhaustion that art collecting is a phenomenon of the decadent. And in moments of puritan reaction people give it up. In any case there comes a moment when the sacrifices reach the point of diminishing returns. Moreover, the aesthete is often fatally attracted to the violent; and, on the principle that rapists are usually invited, positively wants the wrecker to shatter his private universe, hoping, once he is free of things, to be free himself.

Something of this kind seems to be happening in America where we watch the discomfort of the President and the discomfort of the Museum for the same set of reasons. Ever since the priest bureaucracies of Ancient Egypt and Mesopotamia, the upper classes have put precious objects into depositaries. The extent of the treasure proves symbolically the power of the Tribe, City or State. For power is always manifested by the capacity of authority to hold wealth. The American Museum became a paraphrase of the State itself, with its ceremonial unveilings, presentations of wealth heavily guarded, its technical experts and providers of cash, its court of privileged visitors and the not-so privileged public for whose education the Museum ostensibly exists. But education, as defined by a former director of the Metropolitan in New York, is the 'art of casting false pearls before real swine'. It frequently aims to teach people the full extent of their ignorance.

For many years the American Museum publicly demonstrated the power of money; it became more splendid as the cities became more squalid. To some eyes the recent embellishment of the Metropolitan appeared to defy the poverty programme of the City's administration, but the old cry, 'We can't eat stones,' was deflected and ignored. The new wing of the Cleveland Museum, designed by Marcel Breuer, is not so much an exhibition space as a fortified bunker. It is of some psychological interest that the more exquisite the Oriental objects it houses, the further they are buried underground in black stone crypts, while in the park outside, trees and children gasp for air, and streams and ponds are oily black and perhaps inflammable.

Such observable disparities turned people against art, particularly valuable art. The artists started it by creating unsaleable nothings. Now they have been joined by a chorus of critics, who once jumped on the art wagon and find it convenient to jump off. A famous New York critic declared the other day that, in his experience, people who are attracted to art are – it goes without saying – *psychopaths*, unable to tell the difference between right and wrong.

Why psychopath? Because, in some opinions, the work of art is a source of pleasure and power, the object of fetishistic adoration, which serves in a traumatised individual as a substitute for skin-to-skin contact with the mother, once denied, like the kisses of Proust's mother, in early childhood. Art objects, leather gear, rubber goods, boots, frillies, or the vibrating saddle, all compensate for having lost 'mama en chemise toute nue'.

The word 'fetish' derives from a Portuguese expression, *fetiçio*; it carries implications of being a thing magical or enchanted, with an additional meaning of something embellished or false, like *maquillage*. The term 'fetishism' was first employed by a very acute Frenchman called the Président de Brosses in 1760, who described 'the cult, perhaps not less ancient than the cult of stars, of certain earthly material objects called fetishes by Black Africans. I shall call this cult fetishism. Even if in its original context it pertains to the beliefs of Blacks, I intend to use it for any nation whose sacred objects are animals or inanimate things endowed with some divine virtue.' He added that the things varied from a statue to a tree, a cow, a lion's tail, a stone, a shell, or the sea itself. Each was less than God, but possessed of some spirit that made it worthy of adoration.

The Président de Brosses was a figure of the Enlightenment. He frowned on this childish adoration of fetishes. And he failed, of course, to notice in his own colonial civilisation a mania for profits that carried fetishism one step further in infantility. Other writers on fetishism included Auguste Comte, for whom it was a religious phase through which all races had to pass; for Hegel it was a condition in which the poor Blacks were stuck; for Karl Marx 'the fetishism of the commodity' was inseparable from bourgeois capitalism but would evaporate into communistic harmony once the working masses had possessed themselves of the things of the rich. And finally we come to Freud who said that the fetishistic attachment to things was rooted in the psychopathology of the individual, was, in effect, a perversion, and as a perversion could be cured.

Freud said something very original and very profound about fetishism. If we could fathom the depths of its profundity, we might either discover it to be meaningless or to answer all our economic woes and moral dilemmas. He said, 'The fetish is a substitute for the phallus of the mother which the child does not want to relinquish.' And he also said, 'These substitutes can meaningfully be compared to the fetiches in which the savage incarnates his god.' Thus he implied that the savage's adoration of sticks, stones, cows or the sea follows exactly the same psychological process as attachment to Meissen figures, kelims or motor bikes. Even if I understood it better, I cannot hope to expound the convolutions of Freud's complexes and his contention that all fetishism has at root a horror of the sexual organs of the opposite sex. But we should note in passing that he does raise a fascinating insight into why, from the ancient Siberian shaman to the modern artist, the creator is likely to have sex problems; and why men, who notoriously have greater difficulties in their relations with their mothers, have produced more and greater artists than women. And when he remarks on the fetishist's heightened sensitivity to touch, we are forcibly reminded of Mr Berenson's 'tactile values'.

Instead of immersing ourselves in Freud, I suggest we accept as fact that a human infant requires the immediate and constant presence of its mother and her breast for at least the first fifteen months of its life. If this presence is withdrawn and the child pawned off with substitutes for the mother, the results will not necessarily be fatal, but will produce a different sort of character. The Harlows, a team of animal behaviourists, studied rhesus monkeys and found that if their clinging reflexes were directed solely towards inanimate objects, such as a mechanical mother, they grew up drastically disturbed in their sociability – withdrawn, morose, perverted, and hopelessly selfish. And Dr John Bowlby of the Tavistock Clinic found a similar pattern in children left by their mothers. If a very young child, whose bonds of attachment to its mother were firmly cemented, was taken from her, it would cry inconsolably at first and pass into sullen despair, but then, quite suddenly, it would brighten up and take an intelligent interest in its surroundings – and in particular in *things*, teddy bears, rattles, sweets, or any sort of amusement. This lively upsurge of interest always causes relief to the guardians of the child, because it has apparently recovered from the absence of the mother. In fact Bowlby maintains that irreparable damage has been done, for when the mother returns, although the child greets her cheerfully, it does so with a glazed aloofness, as the provider of more things to keep it amused. If this is so, the child that plays happily with its toys is meat for fetishistic activity later, and the prototype of the thing-fixed citizen of today. The playpen will be civilisation's cage in microcosm.

But why the intensity of the bond? Why must all small children stick close by their mothers? Why must they rapidly come unstuck from them if they are to mature? If one examines this question in terms of living in a city or even a mud hut, one does not arrive at the answer. Instead I would ask you to accept that all our emotions have a function in nature, but before they begin to make sense, we must first cross-reference them with the original habitat of early man. I also ask you to take it that our species evolved in a temperate climate (which is why we are hairless); that we were hunters of game animals and gatherers of vegetable food; that seasonal challenge forced on us annual migrations (which is why we have the long striding walk unknown to our primate cousins and why we symbolise life as a long journey); that our hands developed to make our essential equipment – the slings and spears, axes and baskets without which we should be lost; that ideally a man should own no possessions but those he can conveniently carry; that the basic unit of human sociability was *not* the hunting band, but the group united in defence against the zoological monstrosities with which we shared the bush (for this alone will explain why children are expert palaeozoologists in their night-mares, and why the prime object of our hate is always a beast or a bestialised man); and finally that this archaic life, for all its danger *was* the Golden Age for which we preserve an instinctive nostalgia and to which we would mentally return. Today Serengeti is innocuous compared to the dangers it contained in the Early Pleistocene, but if a mother left her child alone there, I doubt if she would find it alive twenty minutes later. In the context of the African savannahs we shall understand the function of the child's clinging: that the mother's breast is not simply the source of food, but something to hang on to; that when a squalling infant has to be walked back to happiness it demands to be on its mother's left side as she herself walked on her daily migration; that the desperate screams for help are protests against abandonment (for when a mother leaves her child she murders it); and that when it gives her a cool reception later, it is simply exacting revenge. We will also understand why, in the light of future dangers facing him, a boy must learn to break away from the mother and stand, to use a cliché, on his own two feet.

But why the attachment to things? Is the work of art really a compensation against abandonment? The Freudian notion of fetishism is fine if you favour a Nothing But philosophy. But it doesn't really get us very far. It may help fathom some of the more obsessive collecting manias. But the acquisition of symbolic things cannot really be a perversion, because everybody does it, deprivation trauma or no. And if the behaviour of their so-called 'primitive' descendants is anything to go by, the earliest men spent much of their time bargaining, bartering, giving and receiving things which were formally useless with the same enthusiasm and irrationality as the modern art collector.

Art, like language, is a communication system. But unlike language it overrides linguistic and cultural barriers. Show an Eskimo a Velazquez and he will ignore it at first. But he can also learn to master its finer points far quicker than he can the sonnets of Gongora. 'Art', as Chesterton once said, 'is the signature of man.' Moreover, an art style is the signature of a particular man and a window on to the age in which he made it.

When I studied prehistoric archaeology we were encouraged to examine the objects of the past, to measure them, compare them to others, and date them. But when one speculated on the character and the beliefs of their makers, such inferences were frowned on as speculative, emotional and unscientific. Unhappily for the prehistorian, prehistoric religion is irrecoverable. It is for him a non-problem, not meriting his attention. But the position is not so desperate. Thanks to Rorschach and other tests we are beginning to be able to determine the character, or psychic life, of a man by the things he makes or even likes. The art object is what psychologists call a cognitive map, which reveals more about the artist than he would ever care to reveal.

I have harped on the connection between art and sex. And the first thing to remember is that the sexes have very different ways of seeing things. Societies simpler than our own have always made the distinction between male and female property, between *his* and *her* things; the Married Women's Property Act would have been a non sequitur. Certainly in other periods it is usually possible to decide which sex made what. Alone the twentieth century would reveal a pattern of total mixed-upness.

At this point let us also recall that early man did not know the existence of a neuter, inert thing. For him everything in the universe was mysteriously alive and sending messages. Stones and trees have often spoken to mystics like Mohammed or to depressives like Gérard de Nerval. And if the universe was alive it was also sexed. The subconscious appears to contain a mechanism for dividing the world of our experience into sexed opposites, male and female, corresponding to the Chinese Yin and Yang. Mountains, rocks and promontories are likely to be male; caves, crevasses and bays female. The sky raining thunderbolts and covering the earth is always male. The Earth is always the Mother. One cannot with certainty predict the sex of, say, the sun. For Louis XIV the Sun was male and symbolised potency, light over darkness, order over chaos, power and glory. For the Rwala Bedouin of Arabia the sun is a mean and destructive old hag, who forces the handsome moon to sleep with her once a month, and so exhausts him that he needs another month to recover. The point to notice is that everything is sexed one way or the other; and the archaic languages preserve this. Hebrew contains no neuter, and the French have preserved 'la chose'.

The sexing of things applies equally to man-made objects. A Scottish psychologist examined some admirably normal school children and found that boys have a taste for soft rounded objects, while the girls favour linear ones, developing a marked taste for the hard and cylindrical as they reach puberty. And if one applies this insight to art styles, one would hope to be able to identify the periods in which the women were sexually secure, finding correspondences in the exuberant heterosexuality of a Rubens and the curves of a Neolithic figurine. Conversely in a man-dominated society (where women are denigrated or denied), we should expect a linear purity in art. And we find it in the rigid verticals of the Greek Doric Order, the Islamic minaret, Cistercian architecture, or the art of the Shakers.

Tricky ground, but apparently we can go further. It seems that abstract designs, preferably symmetrical with plenty of open space, are the artistic expression of anarchic societies in which social differences, if they exist, are tacitly ignored. And if you don't place one man over another, you don't seem to place one species over another. Accordingly, one finds that people who do not elevate themselves above the rest of nature incline to an abstract art. If this is so, it is rather surprising that the people who have been called the 'Nature-Folk' should deny nature in their art; and it will cause terrible headaches for interpreters of Palaeolithic cave painting. However, it will very conveniently explain the nomad's horror of the image, and why bouts of iconoclasm are the peculiar feature of all millenarian or levelling movements.

The reverse proposition also seems to hold true. Devotion to images increases within a hierarchy where everyone knows his place on the ladder and where man elevates himself above other species. Certainly we can trace an affinity between the Lion Kings of Assyria, God Almighty as Pantokrator in a Byzantine apse, or Lenin and Marx raised to superhuman proportions in Red Square. All of these images mesmerise their beholders into submission to higher authority. Researchers have also claimed that a tendency to view human figures in profile betokens a shifting, oblique view of life, and of course one can go on like this indefinitely.

I will now ask you to accept that a work of art is a metaphorical affirmation of territory, and an expression of the people who live there. An African ancestor statue, not less than a Gainsborough, announces the legitimacy of a man, family or tribe in their own particular place. Now we have all heard the notion that art collecting is territory formation. The collector patterns his spot as a dog marks a round of lamp-posts. And we shall speculate that man's fixation with things, which Freud branded as a perversion, is simply his means of marking a place in which to live. Things appear to be vital to us; to be without them is to be lost or deranged.

The late Professor Winnicott had another name for the fetish. He called it a 'transitional object'. For our children, this object might be a teddy bear, the corner of a sheet, or a piece of wood. Winnicott maintained that the child must be allowed to play with things; otherwise it will never form its own personal space and break away from the mother to orientate itself to the outside world.

If the practice of the 'primitives' is anything to go by, Winnicott is right. Mothers of Bushmen children give them the whole inventory of the land in which they will grow up. The child fingers, sniffs and bites shells, flowers, animals, stones or fungi. As he learns to speak he patterns his discoveries into a sequence of metaphorical associations, comparing like and like, and thus forms an ideal territory in his mind. It is significant that the people who speak the most complex languages in the world are the best oriented to their territory. Charles Darwin nearly took the Yaghan Indians of Tierra del Fuego for a sub-human species; yet one of their boys could speak as many words as Shakespeare ever wrote. But they were never allowed by their mothers to hoard things, merely to handle them and let them go. Gypsies, I would add, do not have toys.

The scene of our childhood explorations resides in our minds as a lost paradise which we are always trying to recapture. Proust's description of the Jardin du Pré-Catalan at Illiers is the consummate example in literature. But the savage never outgrows his infantile paradise unless he is forcibly expelled from it. And I suspect that all the time and effort we spend in making or wanting new things (which we have ritualised as the Myth of Progress) merely compensates for the ideal territory from which we have estranged ourselves. Only at our roots can we hope for a renewal. The Australian Aborigines would wander afield throughout the year but return at seasonal intervals to their sacred places to make contact with their ancestral roots, established in the 'dreamtime'. And I once met a man who did the same.

I had felt estranged from my friends and enjoyed the company of a man who was very old and very wise in Islamic teaching. He was also the commercial attaché of a Middle Eastern embassy. One evening there came to his flat in Victoria an Englishman of about fifty-five with an expression of perfect composure. No wrinkle lined him. He seemed to belong to that nearly extinct species – the happy man. He was not withdrawn or half out of this world, but very much in it. Yet he lived a life which would reduce most of us to nervous breakdowns. He was the representative of a manufacturer of typewriters and every three months he visited nearly all the countries of Africa by plane. He had no relatives or attachments. He lived from a suitcase, and the suitcase was sufficently small to fit under the seat of an aeroplane so that he could carry it as hand baggage. When he passed through London he renewed the lot, the suitcase and the clothes. He appeared to possess nothing else, but when I pressed him he admitted to owning a box which he didn't want to discuss. I would make fun of him, he said. I promised not to laugh at the box, and he told me he kept in the office safe a solicitor's black tin deed box. Inside it were his *things*. Back in London four times a year he would sleep in the office bunk room which the company reserved for its travelling salesmen. For half an hour he would lock the door, take the things from the box and spread them on the bunk. They were the assorted bric-à-brac of English middle-class life – the teddy bear, the photograph of his father killed in the First War, his medal, the letter from the King, some of his mother's trinkets, a swimming trophy and a presentation ashtray. But each time he brought from Africa one new thing, and he threw out one old thing that had lost its meaning. 'I know it sounds silly,' he said, 'but they are my roots.' He is the only man I have ever met who solved the tricky equation between things and freedom. The box was the hub of his migration orbit, the territorial fixed point at which he could renew his identity. And without it he would have become literally deranged.

If *things* are territorial markers, we should remind ourselves of the function of territory in species other than our own. A territory is the tract of land an animal and its group needs to feed and breed in. Among baboons, dominant males defend their frontiers until they give way to a more powerful newcomer. Their instinctive fighting apparatus serves two distinct functions: one to protect females and the children from wild beasts; the other to maintain fitness in the Darwinian sense, by preventing inferior males from breeding and contributing their inferiority to the gene pool. For an animal without territory may become sterile.

Now man is certainly equipped to kill other animals for food and defend himself against dangerous beasts. Our adrenal system alone confirms this. But instead of beating his neighbouring rivals into submission, he maintained fitness by the Incest Taboo. He distinguished his own group from outsiders, the in-group from the out-group. The out-group lived in the territory which provided his women, and they alone were sexually permitted to him. He had to define a frontier between *his* and *her* territory. And he did so by fighting for it, not with fists, but with things. He made ritual exchanges of useless gifts that were no less aggressive than an armed scuffle. These things (necessarily sexed) were, like our works of art, statements of territorial integrity, and were used for the moral purpose of diplomacy. We all know that gift-giving is aggressive, and can observe it in the custom whereby heads of state, who cordially loathe each other, nevertheless present each other with idiotic ornaments.

We frequently read blustering letters on the erosion of Britain's art treasures. The sale of a Velazquez to the Metropolitan generates more heat in the press than the sale of some vast industrial complex to overseas investors. For some irrational reason, the sale of a Velazquez is the loss of a symbol, while the sale of a company obeys normal economic pressures. Imagine the upheaval if the Metropolitan bought the Crown Jewels. America would have absorbed Britain and destroyed our territorial integrity. But if we lent the Crown Jewels and borrowed the Declaration of Independence, albeit a bad deal, it would be seen as a reciprocal act of goodwill between two rival, but friendly, nations. It is precisely such tit-for-tat dealing in symbolic things, on the basis of one-to-one parity, that makes people friendly, or at least makes them feel that they are not being taken advantage of. Property, to quote Proudhon, may be theft; but if we remove all property we remove the social cement which keeps people at peace. When the delicate balance of ownership and exchange is upset, men begin to fight. And if gift-giving without due return is aggressive, it is not surprising that the dog bites the hand which feeds it.

We often imagine all trade to be a system of regulating the flow of necessities. Our banking credits are variations on a 'natural' economy of barter in which I exchange my eggs for your turnips, so that we both eat eggs and turnips. If we believe this, we will also believe that the art market has imposed itself as a by-product of this natural economy, and is mere surplus and frivolity. However, this does not prevent businessmen thinking of the money market as an irrational game. And if we care to look at the behaviour of savages, we find no 'natural' economy, no primitive communism where everything is shared, but a great part of life taken up in hard-headed deals and selfish bargaining in *useless things*. For the trade of territorial symbols precedes the exchange of commodities. In the Trobriand Islands two villages traded with each other in yams, despite the fact they were both well supplied with identical yams. The yams were chosen because they were pretty yams, not because they were better to eat. The point being, that if I invade you with my pretty yams, I have a territorial claim on you, and I must expect you to invade me with even prettier yams if we are going to remain at peace.

It will be an honour for me to receive a pretty but useless thing from you. But it will be dangerous for me to hoard it and gloat over it. If I do, I will attract the envy I wish to avoid. Also the *thing* itself, is alive. It does not like being trapped and longs to return to its roots (and having got there to take off again). Instead I will pass the thing on to someone else over whom I wish to have a moral hold. Then one day he will be forced to give me another pretty thing and I will pass it on to you. I know that if I am generous with my things, I will attract more things from my friends – only please God they have good taste! This is a rather different morality of things, and what we should, in an ideal world, be doing with our art collections. All the same, it's nice to think that something like the art market existed before the bankers.

1973

NOTES

I HORREUR DU DOMICILE

The title of this section is taken from one of Chatwin's favourite quotations: 'La grande maladie de l'horreur du domicile', from Baudelaire's *Journaux intimes*. The phrase recurs frequently throughout his work, becoming a sort of leitmotif, most notably in *The Songlines*.

'I Always Wanted to Go to Patagonia – The Making of a Writer' was published in the *New York Times Book Review*, 2 August 1983: pp. 6, 34–6

'A Place to Hang Your Hat' is a description of one of Chatwin's principal 'writer's chambers' – his pied-à-terre in London – and an exploration of the author's paradoxical attitude to home. It was written for *House & Garden* to draw attention to the work of the flat's designer, the architect John Pawson.

'A Tower in Tuscany' evokes another of the 'writer's chambers': Gregor von Rezzori's mediaeval signalling tower, near Florence. Chatwin liked to write 'away from home' while staying with friends such as von Rezzori in Italy, Patrick Leigh Fermor in Greece, or George Melly in Wales, in whose tower overlooking the River Usk he was to write part of *On the Black Hill*.

The title 'Gone to Timbuctoo' echoes the famous telegram of resignation that Chatwin is said to have sent to the *Sunday Times* in 1975 on leaving for Patagonia: 'Gone to Patagonia for Six Months'. The article was originally published in *Vogue*, in 1970. (See also N. Murray *Bruce Chatwin*, Seren Books, Bridgend, 1993, pp. 38–9, for an account of this episode.)

II STORIES

In his introduction to *What Am I Doing Here*, Chatwin wrote: 'The word "story" is intended to alert the reader to the fact that, however closely the narrative may fit the facts, the fictional process has been at work.' The following selection of 'stories' reveals how fact and fiction fuse under Chatwin's pen to emerge as a single seamless narrative.

'Milk', a tale of initiation clearly drawn from Chatwin's African notebooks, was published in the *London Magazine*, August–September 1977 (and was later reprinted in *London Magazine Stories*, in 1979).

'The Attractions of France' was published posthumously by the Colophon Press in 1993. The original typescript is undated and was only discovered after the author's death. It is the fictionalised account of a true-life episode taken from the notebooks. Chatwin was an avowed francophile; the title reflects his admiration for French literature and culture.

In 'The Estate of Maximilian Tod', Chatwin explores the psychology of the obsessive collector: an autobiographical theme he was to return to in 'The Morality of Things', before making it the central concern of his last novel, *Utz*, some ten years later.

Significantly, *Tod* is the German word for 'death'. The story appeared in the *Saturday Night Reader*, W. H. Allen, in 1979.

'Bedouins' is possibly the shortest and most succinct of the author's anecdotal tales, or 'miniatures'. Chatwin relates a different version of the same story in the 'Notebooks' section of *The Songlines*, pp. 211–12.

III 'THE NOMADIC ALTERNATIVE'

This section brings together three separate texts which explore the nature of nomadism. Taken together, they are perhaps the closest one can come to an idea of what the author's 'unpublishable' book on nomads may have looked like, had it seen the light of day. According to a footnote attached to the third text, 'It's a nomad *nomad* World', the book was due to be published by Jonathan Cape in 1971. Chatwin makes repeated allusions to the manuscript throughout his work, although he seems subsequently to have destroyed it.

'Letter to Tom Maschler'. This previously unpublished letter, dating from 1968, was written in response to the editor's request for a synopsis of Chatwin's planned book on nomads. It resulted in a book contract with Jonathan Cape which was later transferred to the manuscript of *In Patagonia*, once the original project had been abandoned. Chatwin's 'nomad letter' prefigures a series of texts on the same theme that appeared in various periodicals in the early 1970s.

Untypically for the author, the letter is typewritten and bears a handwritten postscript: '*Sorry, I have a fiendish typewriter.*'

'The Nomadic Alternative' is Chatwin's principal contribution to *Animal Style (Art from East to West)*, the catalogue of an archaeological exhibition of nomad art-work which he helped organise in New York in 1970. Controversial in nature, the essay appears to have been deliberately relegated to the end of the catalogue. The 'Letter to Tom Maschler' suggests that it was to have been one of the main chapters of Chatwin's nomad book.

The final article in this section, a summary of Chatwin's key ideas on the subject of nomadism, was originally published under the title: 'It's a nomad nomad nomad NOMAD world' in the December 1970 issue of *Vogue*. A footnote links the article to the author's ambitious book project: 'Bruce Chatwin, an insatiable wanderer himself, is now compiling a book on nomadism to be published by Jonathan Cape in 1971.'

IV REVIEWS

Bruce Chatwin's reviews figure among the least known of his writings. The texts gathered together here reveal a critic possessed of strongly held views at times bordering on the polemical. While the author displays a marked penchant for the play of 'grand ideas' in his reviews, his narrative technique is also well to the fore in texts like 'The Anarchists of Patagonia', which reads like a blueprint for the 'Revolution' chapter in *In Patagonia*.

'Abel the Nomad', a critical review of Wilfred Thesiger's *Desert, Marsh and Mountain* (Collins, London), was published in *The London Review of Books*, 22 November 1979, p. 9. In eulogistic terms, Chatwin reveals his natural affinity with the compulsive wanderer in Thesiger. The myth of Abel and Cain is a recurrent 'motif' in Chatwin's œuvre, notably in *The Viceroy of Ouidah* and *The Songlines*.

'The Anarchists of Patagonia' is a review of Osvaldo Bayer's three-volume *Los Vengadores de la Patagonia Trágica* (Editorial Galerna, Buenos Aires). It was published in *The Times Literary Supplement*, 31 December 1976, pp. 1635–6. In keeping with his belief in the indivisibility of fact and fiction, Chatwin resorts to the techniques of fictional narrative to relate an extravagant episode in Patagonian history.

'The Road to the Isles' is a critical review of James Pope-Hennessy's biography of Robert Louis Stevenson, published in *The Times Literary Supplement*, 25 October 1974, pp. 1195–6.

'Variations on an Idée Fixe' is a review of Konrad Lorenz's *The Year of the Greylag Goose* (Harcourt Brace Jovanovich/a Helen and Kurt Wolff book), published in the *New York Review of Books*, 6 December 1979, pp. 8–9. Later, Chatwin was to discuss Lorenz's behaviourist ideas at length in the 'Notebooks' section of *The Songlines*, presenting them as an antithesis to his own theory of nomadism.

V ART AND THE IMAGE–BREAKER

Chatwin came closest to formulating a comprehensive statement of his aesthetics when writing about the fine arts. The following texts discuss the decadence of Western art, and in doing so mark a vigorous counterpoint to the author's previous career as art expert and collector.

With its pantheon of extravagant characters, finely wrought descriptive passages and irreverent humour, 'Among the Ruins' is a characteristically 'Chatwinian' tale of modern decadence, originally published in *Vanity Fair*, April 1984, pp. 46–60, under the fuller – and more explicit – title: 'Self-Love Among the Ruins'.

'The Morality of Things', originally sub-titled 'A Talk by Bruce Chatwin', is the typescript of a speech that Chatwin gave at a Red Cross charitable art auction in 1973. It was published posthumously, in a limited private press edition, by Robert Risk (Typographeum, New Hampshire) in 1993. The text explores the philosophical and psychological implications of possession, a subject Chatwin was to return to in narrative form in his last novel, *Utz*.

BIBLIOGRAPHY

PRINCIPAL WORKS

In Patagonia, London: Jonathan Cape, 1977, 204 pp. (Paperback edition – London: Picador, 1979, 189 pp.)

The Viceroy of Ouidah, London: Jonathan Cape, 1980, 155 pp. (Paperback edition – London: Picador, 1982, 126 pp.)

On the Black Hill, London: Jonathan Cape, 1982, 284 pp. (Paperback edition – London: Picador, 1983, 249 pp.)

Patagonia Revisited (text by Bruce Chatwin and Paul Theroux; illustrations by Kyffin Williams), Salisbury: Michael Russel, 1985, 62 pp. (Reprinted by Jonathan Cape, London, 1992, 62 pp.) (U.S. edition: *Nowhere is a place: travels in Patagonia* [text by Bruce Chatwin and Paul Theroux; photographs by Jeff Gnass; introduction by Paul Theroux], San Francisco: Yolla Bolly Press book, published by Sierra Club Books, 1992, 109 pp.)

The Songlines, London: Jonathan Cape, 1987, 293 pp. (Paperback edition – London: Picador, 1988, 327 pp.)

Utz, London: Jonathan Cape, 1988, 154 pp. (Paperback edition – London: Picador, 1988, 154 pp.)

Bibliography

What Am I Doing Here, London: Jonathan Cape, 1989, 367 pp.
(Paperback edition – London: Pan Books, 1990, 367 pp.)

Photographs and Notebooks, London: Jonathan Cape, 1993, 160 pp.

LIMITED EDITIONS, CATALOGUES AND ANTHOLOGIES

Animal Style (Art from East to West) (Bruce Chatwin with Emma Bunker & Ann Farkas), New York: The Asia Society Inc., 1970, 185 pp.[1]

Great American Families (Bruce Chatwin & various authors), New York, Times Books, 1978, 192 pp.[2]

Cobra Verde: Filmbuch (Werner Herzog). Fotografien von Beat Presser, Tagebuch von Bruce Chatwin, Gespräche mit Werner Herzog von Steff Gruber, Geschichte des Films und Dialoge von Werner Herzog. Schaffhausen: Edition Stemmle, 1987, 152 pp.

John Pawson (Bruce Chatwin & various authors; tr. fr. Spanish by E. Bonet), Spain: Gustavo Gili, 1992, 94 pp.[3]

The Morality of Things – A Talk by Bruce Chatwin, Francestown, New Hampshire: Typographeum, 1993, 26 pp.[4]

---

[1] Distributed by New York Graphic Society.

[2] Bruce Chatwin's contribution is entitled 'The Guggenheim Family': an article first printed in *The Times Literary Supplement* under the title 'The Guggenheim Saga'. Other contributing authors include Gore Vidal, V.S. Pritchett and Edward Jay Epstein.

[3] Part of the series 'Monographs on Contemporary Design'. Bruce Chatwin's contribution is derived from an article he wrote for *House & Garden* in June 1984, entitled 'A Place to Hang your Hat', included in the present volume.

[4] The transcript of a talk delivered by the author for the British Red Cross Society before a charity art auction held in London on 12 June 1973.

Bibliography

The Attractions of France, London: Colophon Press, 1993, 17pp.

Prague, edited by John and Kirsten Miller, San Francisco: Chronicle Books, 1994.[1]

PREFACES, POSTSCRIPTS, ARTICLES AND STORIES

'The Bust of Sekhmet'. In *Ivory Hammer 4: The Year at Sotheby's & Parke-Bernet 1965–66*, London: Longman, 1966, pp. 302–3.[2]

'The Nomadic Alternative'. In Emma Bunker, Bruce Chatwin & Ann Farkas, *Animal Style (Art from East to West)*, New York: The Asia Society Inc., 1970, pp. 175–183.

'Museums'. In Robert Allen & Quentin Guirdham (eds), *The London Spy – a discreet guide to the city's pleasures*, London: Blond, 1971, pp. 95–109.[3]

'The Estate of Maximilian Tod'. In Emma Tennant (ed.), *Saturday Night Reader*, London: W. H. Allen, 1979, pp. 25–37.[4]

'Foreword'. In Lorenzo Ricciardi, *The Voyage of the Mir-el-lah*, London: Collins, 1980, p. 6.

'Introduction'. In Robert Byron, *The Road to Oxiana*, London: Pan Books, 1981. pp. 9–15.[5]

---

[1] A collection of previously published literary works and excerpts by Havel, Kafka, Chatwin, Jirásek, Bachmann, Škvorecký.
[2] The first article known to have been published by the author.
[3] Unsigned.
[4] Also printed in the American review *Triquarterly n° 46*, Fall 1979, pp. 43–56.
[5] Reprinted in *What Am I Doing Here* under the title 'A Lament for Afghanistan', pp. 286–93.

'Howard Hodgkin'. In Michael Compton, *Howard Hodgkin's Indian Leaves*, London: Tate Gallery catalogue, 1982.[1]

'Body and Eyes'. In Robert Mapplethorpe, *Lady: Lisa Lyon*, New York: Viking Press, 1983, pp. 11–15.[2]

'Introduction'. In Osip Mandelstam, *Journey to Armenia*, London: Redstone Press, 1989, pp.4–7.

'Introduction'. In Sybil Bedford, *A Visit to Don Otavio*, London: Folio Society, 1990, pp.11–12.

CONTRIBUTIONS TO PERIODICALS

'Gone to Timbuctoo'. In *Vogue*, July 1970, pp. 20, 22, 25.[3]

'It's a Nomad Nomad Nomad NOMAD world'. In *Vogue*, December 1970, pp. 124–5.

'The Mechanics of Nomad Invasions'. In *History Today*, 22 May 1972, pp. 329–37 + bibliography, p. 382.[4]

'Surviving in Style'. In the *Sunday Times* magazine, 4 March 1973, pp. 42–54.[5]

[1] Later included in *What Am I Doing Here*, pp. 70–8. Published to accompany an exhibition held at the Tate Gallery in London from 22 September to 7 November 1982.

[2] Reprinted from the *Sunday Times* magazine: published in the UK as 'An Eye and Somebody'. In Robert Mapplethorpe, *Lady Lisa Lyon*, London: Blond & Briggs, 1983, 128 pp.

[3] Reprinted in the *Vogue Bedside Book* (edited by Jonathan Ross), London: Vermilion, 1984, 256 pp.

[4] Reprinted as 'Nomad Invasions'. In *What Am I Doing Here*, pp. 329–37.

[5] Featuring articles on Madeleine Vionnet (reprinted in *What Am I Doing Here*, pp. 86–93) and Sonia Delaunay.

'Moscow's Unofficial Art'. In the *Sunday Times* magazine, May 6 1973, pp. 36–54.[1]

'Postscript to a Thousand Pictures', the *Sunday Times* magazine, 26 August 1973, pp. 48–51.[2]

'Heavenly Horses'. In the *Sunday Times* magazine, 9 September 1973, pp. 56–61.[3]

'Fatal Journey to Marseilles – North Africans in France'. In the *Sunday Times* magazine, 6 January 1974, pp. 22–45.[4]

'The Oracle'. In the *Sunday Times* magazine, 17 March 1974, pp. 20–34.[5]

'The Witness'. In the *Sunday Times* magazine, 9 June 1974, pp. 52–9.[6]

'The Road to the Isles'. In *The Times Literary Supplement*, no. 3790, 25 October 1974, pp. 1195–6.

'Man the Aggressor'. In the *Sunday Times* magazine, 1 December 1974, pp. 28–41, 85–7.[7]

---

[1] Reprinted in *What Am I Doing Here* under the title 'George Costakis: The Story of an Art Collector in the Soviet Union', pp. 153–169.

[2] The postscript to a series on the history of art entitled 'One Million Years of Art' which Chatwin edited for the *Sunday Times* from 24 June to 26 August 1973.

[3] Reprinted in *What Am I Doing Here*, pp. 195–205.

[4] Reprinted in *What Am I Doing Here* under the title 'The Very Sad Story of Salah Bougrine', pp. 241–68.

[5] Reprinted in *What Am I Doing Here* under the title 'André Malraux', pp. 114–35.

[6] Chatwin's contribution to a magazine feature about occupied Paris entitled 'Life goes on'. It was later rewritten and reprinted as 'An Aesthete at War', in the *New York Review of Books*, 5 March 1981, pp. 21–5.

[7] A profile of Konrad Lorenz, excerpts of which were later included in the 'From the Notebooks' section of *The Songlines*.

'The Riddle of the Pampa'. In the *Sunday Times* magazine, 26 October 1975, pp. 52–67.[1]

'The Guggenheim Saga'. In the *Sunday Times* magazine, 23 November 1975, pp. 34–67.

'The Anarchists of Patagonia'. In *The Times Literary Supplement*, no. 3903, 31 December 1976, pp. 1635–6.

'Milk'. In *London Magazine*, August–September 1977, pp. 40–8.[2]

'Until My Blood Is Pure'. In *Bananas*, no.9, Winter 1977, pp. 10–11.

'Perils of the Israeli Settlement'. In the *Spectator*, 8 April 1978, pp. 8–9.

'Western Approaches'. In the *Radio Times*, 22 June 1978, p. 70.

'A Memory of Nadezhda Mandelstam' and 'An Introduction to Journey to Armenia'. In *Bananas*, no.11, Summer 1978, p. 5.[3]

'The Quest for the Wolf Children'. In the *Sunday Times* magazine, 30 July 1978, pp. 10–13.[4]

[1] Reprinted in *What Am I Doing Here* under the title 'Maria Reiche', pp. 94–113.

[2] A nine-page story later printed in *London Magazine Stories*. London: London Magazine Editions, 1979.

[3] Respectively reprinted as 'Nadezhda Mandelstam: A Visit' in *What Am I Doing Here*, pp. 83–5, and 'Introduction' in Osip Mandelstam, *Journey to Armenia*, London: Redstone Press, 1989, pp. 4–7.

[4] Reprinted in *What Am I Doing Here* under the title 'Shamdev: The Wolf-Boy', pp. 233–40.

Bibliography

'On the Road with Mrs Gandhi'. In the *Sunday Times* magazine, 27 August 1978, pp. 20–34.[1]

'Bedouins'. In *London Magazine*, November 1978, pp. 58–9.

'The Estate of Maximilian Tod'. In *Triquarterly n°46*, Fall 1979, pp. 143–56.

'Abel the Nomad'. In the *New York Review of Books*, 22 November 1979, p. 9.

'Variations on an Idée Fixe'. In the *New York Review of Books*, 6 December 1979, pp. 8–9

'An Aesthete at War'. In the *New York Review of Books*, 5 March 1981, pp. 21–5.[2]

'Von Rezzori'. In *Vogue*, May 1981, pp. 277, 328.

'Donald Evans'. In the *New York Review of Books*, 14 May 1981, pp. 14–16.

'On the Black Hill'. In *Harpers & Queen*, October 1982, pp. 164, 166, 168.[3]

'A Visit to Wiesenthal'. In the *Observer* magazine, 7 November 1982, pp. 51, 53.

'On Yeti Tracks'. In *Esquire*, 1983.

[1] Reprinted in *What Am I Doing Here*, pp. 316–40.
[2] Later included in *What Am I Doing Here* under the title 'Ernst Jünger: An Aesthete at War', pp. 297–315.
[3] Excerpts from the novel.

Bibliography

'Explorations of the Heart'. In *Vogue*, January 1983, pp. 220–1.[1]

'Body Building Beautiful – Lisa Lyons and Robert Mapplethorpe'. In the *Sunday Times* magazine, 17 April 1983, pp. 30–4.

'I Always Wanted to Go to Patagonia – The Making of a Writer'. In the *New York Times Book Review*, 2 August 1983, pp. 6, 34–6.

'A Coup'. In *Granta no.10: 'Travel Writing'*, Cambridge: Granta Publications Ltd, 1984, pp. 107–26.[2]

'Self-Love Among the Ruins'. In *Vanity Fair*, April 1984, pp. 46–60.

'A Place to Hang your Hat'. In *House & Garden*, June 1984, pp. 140–3.

'Great Rivers of the World: the Volga'. In the *Observer* magazine, June 1984, pp. 16–26.[3]

'Les Apocalypses'. In *Lettre Internationale*, winter 84/85, pp. 3–5.

'Where a Wayfarer Halts her Journey: A Welcoming Home for Sally, Duchess of Westminster'. In *Architectural Digest*, June 1985, pp. 202–9.

'In China, Rock's Kingdom'. In the *New York Times* magazine, 16 March 1986, section 6, part II, pp. 34–47, 104–5, 109.[4]

---

[1] An excerpt from *On the Black Hill*.
[2] Reprinted in *What Am I Doing Here* under the title 'A Coup – A Story', pp. 15–35.
[3] Reprinted as 'The Volga'. In *Great Rivers of the World*, London: Hodder & Stoughton, 1984. Also included in *What Am I Doing Here*, pp. 170–91.
[4] Reprinted in *What Am I Doing Here* as 'Rock's World', pp. 206–15.

Bibliography

'A Tower in Tuscany'. In *House & Garden*, January 1987, pp. 78–85.

'Dreamtime'. In *Granta no. 21: 'The Story-Teller'*, Cambridge: Granta Publications Ltd, Spring 1987, pp. 39–79.[1]

'The Lizard Man'. In the *New York Review of Books*, 13 August 1987, pp. 47–8.[2]

'In Natasha's Trunk'. In the *New York Review of Books*, 24 September 1987, pp. 17–18.[3]

'The Albatross'. In *Granta no. 24*, 1988, pp. 11–13.

'Chiloe'. In *Granta no. 24*, 1988, pp. 166–70.

'When the Revolution Came Home'. In *House & Garden*, January 1988, pp. 122–5.[4]

'On Location. Gone to Ghana: the making of Werner Herzog's Cobra Verde'. In *Interview*, March 1988, pp. 82–5.[5]

'Excerpts from the Songlines'. In *Aperture no.11*, Spring 1988, pp. 58–9.

'The Seventh Day – a story by Bruce Chatwin'. In *London Review of Books*, 2 June 1988, p. 13.

---

[1] An excerpt from *The Songlines*.
[2] An excerpt from *The Songlines*.
[3] A Review of Michael Ignatieff's novel *The Russian Album* (New York: Viking/Elisabeth Sifton Books, 1987).
[4] Reprinted in *What Am I Doing Here* under the title 'Konstantin Melnikov: Architect', pp. 105–13.
[5] Reprinted as 'Werner Herzog in Ghana' in *What Am I Doing Here*, pp. 136–49.

Bibliography

'The Songlines Quartet'. In the *New York Review of Books*, 19 January 1989, pp. 50–1.[1]

'Songs of a Friend for Life'. In *The Times*, 20 January 1989, p. 16.[2]

'The Bey', 'Mrs Mandelstam', 'Konstantin Melnikov: Architect', *Granta no. 26: 'Travel'*, Cambridge: Granta Publications Ltd, Spring 1989, pp. 107–25.[3]

'The Duke of M——; My Modi; The Bey'. In the *Daily Telegraph* (weekend section), 6 May 1989, pp. 1–2.[4]

'Your Father's Eyes Are Blue Again'. In the *Observer*, 7 May 1989, p. 45.[5]

'Brief Interludes'. In *Vogue*. August 1989, pp. 326–7.[6]

'On George Ortiz'. In the *New York Review of Books*, 28 September 1989, p. 62.[7]

'The Road to Ouidah'. In *Granta no. 44*, Spring 1993, pp. 223–34.[8]

[1] Excerpt from *What Am I Doing Here*.
[2] Reprinted in *What Am I Doing Here* under the title 'Kevin Volans', pp. 63–9.
[3] Excerpts from *What Am I Doing Here*.
[4] Excerpts from *What Am I Doing Here*.
[5] Excerpt from *What Am I Doing Here*.
[6] Contains the following excerpts from *What Am I Doing Here*: 'At Dinner with D. Vreeland'; 'The Duke of M——'; 'My Modi'.
[7] Excerpt from *What Am I Doing Here*.
[8] A slightly abridged version of the chapter 'The Road to Ouidah' in *Photographs and Notebooks*.

SELECTED INTERVIEWS

'Bruce Chatwin: from Patagonia to the slave trade' (with Mary Blume). In the *International Herald Tribune*, 1980, p. 7.

'In search of the giant sloth and other stories' (with Maureen Cleave). In the *Observer* magazine, 31 October 1982, pp. 32–3.

'Bruce Chatwin' (with Melvyn Bragg). In *The South Bank Show*, London Weekend Television, 7 November 1982.

'An interview with Bruce Chatwin' (with Michael Ignatieff). In *Granta no. 21: 'The Story-teller'*, Cambridge: Granta publications Ltd, Spring 1987, pp. 23–37.

'Heard Between the Songlines' (with Michael Davie). In the *Observer*, 21 June 1987, p. 18.

'Songs of the Earth' (with Lucy Hughes-Hallett). In the *London Evening Standard*, 24 June 1987, p. 33.

'Born Under a Wandering Star' (with Colin Thubron). In the *Daily Telegraph* (weekend section), 27 June 1987, p. 1.

'Bruce Chatwin' (with Michele Field). In *Publishers' Weekly*, 7 August 1987, pp. 430–1.

FILMOGRAPHY

Adaptations
On the Black Hill, by Andrew Grieve (director & scriptwriter), British Film Institute/Film Four International, 1987.

Cobra Verde (adapted from *The Viceroy of Ouidah*), directed & scripted by Werner Herzog, Werner Herzog Filmproduktion, 1990.

Utz, directed by George Sluizer & scripted by Hugh Whitemore, Viva Pictures Ltd, 1992.

Documentaries
'Nach Patagonien (Zu Bruce Chatwins Reise in ein fernes Land)', directed by Jan Schütte, Novoskop Film Jan Schütte, ZDF, 1991.

'Songlines: sur les traces de Bruce Chatwin en Australie', directed by Barbara Dickenberger, Arte, 1993.

PROFILES AND CRITICAL STUDIES OF BRUCE CHATWIN
Peter Levi, *The Light Garden of the Angel King – Journeys in Afghanistan*, London: Collins, 1972, 287 pp .

Nicholas Murray, *Bruce Chatwin*, Bridgend (Wales): Seren Books, 1993, 140 pp.

Claudine Verley (ed.), *B. Chatwin*, Poitiers: les Cahiers forell, no. 4, November 1994, 166 pp.

Alessandro Grassi and Neri Torrigiani (eds), *Bruce Chatwin: Searching for the Miraculous*, Turin: Gruppo GFT, 1995, n. p.

ACKNOWLEDGEMENTS

The editors would like to thank the following individuals and institutions for their help in the preparation of this book:

Pascal Cariss, Susannah Clapp, David Rees, Robert Risk, Francis Wyndham, Cambridge University Library, Jonathan Cape Ltd, la Bibliothèque nationale, The Bodleian Library, The British Council, The British Library, Condé Nast Publications Inc., The Library of Congress.

We are especially grateful to Elizabeth Chatwin and Gillon Aitken for reading and commenting on the manuscript.